Wellbeing Leadership

Wellbeing Leadership

A New Approach for School Leaders

Amy Green

Published in 2024 by Amba Press, Melbourne, Australia
www.ambapress.com.au

© Amy Green 2024

All rights reserved. No part of this book may be reproduced or transmitted in any form or by any means, electronic or mechanical, including photocopying, recording or by any information storage and retrieval system, without prior permission in writing from the publisher.

Cover design: Tess McCabe
Internal design: Amba Press
Editor: Brooke Lyons

ISBN: 9781923215368 (pbk)
ISBN: 9781923215375 (ebk)

A catalogue record for this book is available from the National Library of Australia.

Contents

Preface: A Note to Leaders		v
Introduction		1
Part 1: The Why of Wellbeing Leadership		7
1.	Purpose: *Why Wellbeing Leadership Matters*	11
2.	Past and Present: *Learning from our Mistakes*	31
3.	Priority: *A Wellbeing-Centred Workplace*	43
4.	Perspective: *Knowing Yourself as a Leader*	55
5.	People: *Wellbeing is Culture*	73
Part 2: The How of Wellbeing Leadership		95
6.	Emotional Health	101
7.	Optimism	109
8.	Collective Resilience	119
9.	Meaningful Connection	127
10.	Working Productively	137
11.	Engagement	151
12.	Performance and Growth	159
13.	Psychological Safety	171
Conclusion: Where to Now?		179
References		185
Acknowledgements		189
About the Author		191

Preface: A Note to Leaders

Hey leader,

I'm so glad you have picked up this book. Before you start reading, though, I want to share a few things with you.

I want you to know that you are doing a great job. As leaders, we don't hear this enough. With the weight of so many things falling on our shoulders, we can often underestimate all we have achieved in a day and the impact we have made in a week, month, term or year.

Being a leader is no easy gig. Many of us in leadership roles in education are underprepared and unaware of what's needed to lead well. This isn't our fault. It's a flaw in the system. We often take up leadership roles due to our dedication to education, exceptional ability and expertise as a teacher, and commitment to change. Our passion, enthusiasm and drive, and our desire for things to improve and evolve in our schools, are what inspire us to take the leap from teacher to leader.

However, our teaching degrees haven't prepared us to be leaders. They barely prepared us to be educators. Most of us scrambled our way through our first few years of teaching and put the puzzle pieces together, but becoming a leader is a whole different game.

Right now, post Covid and in the middle of a teacher shortage, leaders must do more than ever before. Not only are we being asked to continue delivering high-quality learning and teaching, and keep up with the increasing administration tasks and system initiatives (which at times we feel like we just get a hold of before they change again), but we have the added layer of wellbeing – for both students and staff.

When I completed my teaching degree, this wasn't something that was made explicit. Student wellbeing was getting some traction, although not as much as it is now, but staff wellbeing was not on the radar at all.

Fast forward nearly two decades and staff wellbeing is now the number one priority for many schools across the globe. This is a great thing. Finally, staff wellbeing is getting the attention and priority it needs.

However, with the new initiative of wellbeing being added to school-improvement agendas and strategic plans, this makes our job as leaders even harder. We know it matters, yet there is very little clarity, consistency or professional development provided to equip us to lead staff wellbeing.

How are we to support the wellbeing of staff when we haven't been given adequate training? When we don't know what staff wellbeing really means? When we don't know who is responsible for what? When we don't know what 'doing it well' looks like?

There is no curriculum for staff wellbeing. There's no shared approach or consistent pedagogy. In some ways this new addition to a leader's job description is completely unknown in expectation. This isn't okay and it's not your fault; but, as a leader, it *is* your responsibility to be open, brave and vulnerable as you lead yourself and your staff in this new phase of teaching and working with wellbeing in mind.

As you read this book I hope you will rethink, question and reflect on your role as leader and who you want to be. When we know things aren't right and something needs to change, we need to be ready to accept our current state, where we may have gone wrong in the past and what we can do now.

As leaders, we have far more autonomy and power than we perhaps realise. We have the ability to be the architects of our schools, designing them to work in ways that support not only our students but our staff, too.

It is time we started to realise this. We need to look through this lens and apply it to our decision-making, change processes and strategic planning. If you do this you will have a school that puts wellbeing at its centre, where staff (including you) thrive and where, as a leader, you feel fulfilled. You'll know that each day you are working with meaning and purpose, supporting yourself and others.

I hope this book gives you a sense of empowerment, that it stretches your perception of what it means to lead with wellbeing at the centre. I hope it opens a door of possibility and prompts you to creatively reflect and rethink.

We have the power to redesign schools as we know they need to be. We can create working environments that not only attract more educators to the profession, but also retain the great people we already have. If we don't start to change now, it may be too late.

Leader, as you read this book I ask you to get excited. I know this may be hard at times and that it can feel like a lot, but we are on the brink of transformation in education, a revolution even, of how we teach, work and lead. It all starts with imagining how we could do things differently.

I hope you are as ready as I am.

Let's do this.

With love and kindness,

Amy

Introduction

I didn't actually set out to become a teacher. While it is the career I fell in love with, and one I am deeply passionate about and miss on a daily basis, it wasn't always my plan.

In my final years of school I prioritised creativity. I immersed myself in art, even skipping a few maths classes to finish a painting or two I was working on (this happened more than once). I embarked on a path that was very different to becoming a teacher. While I eventually made my way to the university building that housed all things education, my initial degree was in Design for Theatre and Television. It was a field I thought would be filled with excitement, fun and adventure. However, after a few months of dreaming up set designs and learning how to rig lights, I realised that the path I was on was not for me. Luckily, switching from theatre design to teaching wasn't that difficult. After filling out a few forms and pleading my case, I was welcomed to teaching and have never looked back.

Teaching turned out to be a career that allowed for excitement, fun and adventure, just not in the same way as climbing up a 3-metre scaffold to hang a disco ball did. There aren't many jobs in which each day is different, you find yourself laughing for the most unexpected reasons and you are literally changing lives and influencing the future.

As a new educator I was filled with the enthusiasm and readiness that you probably remember, too. Even now I can feel the excitement of arriving on the first day and walking into the hall to meet my first-ever class. I was eager: ready to take on any challenge and learn anything that came my way. I put my hand up for just about everything. I was unwaveringly committed to the profession, and those around me started to notice my potential.

By my third year of teaching I was being asked where I saw my career heading. I was still considered an 'early career teacher' at this point. I was by no means an expert in my field, nor did I consider myself a leader. Yet conversations were being had about the next steps for me. Had I considered leadership? How did I feel about being a principal in my early 30s? These conversations came as a surprise to me. While I adored the career I had chosen, I wasn't sure I was ready for such a huge commitment; in fact, I knew I wasn't.

I naturally began to seriously ponder these questions myself. Where did I see myself going? Did I want to be a leader? What about a principal?

I was fortunate to be working with some incredible leaders, so I knew that if I did pursue a leadership path there would be competencies I needed to learn and develop. I also considered that, in my mind, becoming a principal would be 'the end' in terms of my career path. If that's where I end up in my 30s, would I stay there forever? I realised I wasn't quite ready for this leap, or for this type of leadership to be the next step in my career.

I knew I wanted to see something different, though. I wanted to go somewhere different, to learn new things. It was this moment that propelled me to take up a three-year teaching opportunity in London, which coincidentally saw me in various leadership roles.

When I returned to Australia to the same school I had left behind, the leadership path was calling me more strongly than before. I found myself taking up short leadership stints before stepping into a long-term contract as a middle leader.

When I reflect on this, I think it is the natural step for many educators who find themselves in leadership roles. We go from classroom teacher to acting in leadership positions in short timeframes, then on to longer contracts as we wait for a permanent role to become available. While this path looks similar in many schools, there is no denying that not all schools, classrooms or teaching or leadership opportunities are the same. With each school, classroom and student being different, there are many nuances to what you experience day to day, setting to setting. This is both a magical opportunity, and one that makes stepping into leadership challenging.

Working in schools, no matter what your role, places you in a position of service. We give so much to our students, including sacrificing our own wellbeing and energy. When you're a teacher it is always about students. We lose hours designing engaging lessons, lose sleep pondering how to teach better, and continue to question whether what we are doing is enough. As leaders, we worry about all this and more. We are unsure whether the decisions we are making are right, we discuss school priorities and how to do better, and we are always tackling new problems – because in education there are always curveballs.

This continuous pull between priorities and the tendency to give all our energy to being a leader can cause our own wellbeing to dip. It is also why it is hard to connect the dots between our wellbeing and the work we do.

It doesn't matter how much we care for our work, our students, our colleagues and those we lead. It doesn't matter how well-planned our lessons might be, how many items we cross off our to-do list each day, how many staff meetings we deliver or how many strategic plans we create. If we are not actively supporting our own wellbeing – by sleeping, resting, eating nourishing foods, processing and regulating our emotions, building our resilience skills and so much more – we can quickly become overwhelmed. Our wellbeing and how our schools support us to work well are not separate entities; our wellbeing should support the work we do, and our work should support our wellbeing.

This is something that is often misunderstood, or not recognised at all. Working on our wellbeing doesn't mean we do not also look to improve and keep doing our job well. We work in a great profession, and we must continue to be great professionals.

What's missing though is acknowledging that how we work (our systems, structures, processes, timeframes and deadlines, interruptions, workload and competing priorities), how our teams function (team cohesion and collaboration, shared beliefs and values), and how we lead and are led all contribute to wellbeing. Even when we are doing everything we need for our own wellbeing, if these things aren't addressed, we will continue to have staff wellbeing issues. This is the difference between addressing the symptom or the cause.

As you make your way through this book, this is what I hope you take away: the understanding that we can longer address wellbeing only at a symptoms level. We can no longer be reactive or unplanned, or implement loosely considered ad-hoc approaches. Instead, we must give time and space to identify and address the cause of poor wellbeing. We must use data-informed approaches to change, and ideate strategy with all staff contributing to the solution. We must be ready to try, fail, pivot and try again, knowing some things will work and some things won't. Finally, we must understand that the work we are setting ourselves up for is not just addressing staff wellbeing, or even improving culture. Instead, we are redesigning and revolutionising the way schools are run and exist.

In part 1 of this book we will focus on the *why* of wellbeing leadership. We'll look through the lenses of purpose, past and present, priority, perspective and people to discover what wellbeing is, uncover who you are as a leader of wellbeing, and connect staff wellbeing and culture. Part 2 is about the *how* of wellbeing leadership. We'll look at the eight characteristics needed to create a wellbeing-centred workplace where all staff feel, work, team and lead well. Finally we will bring it all together and look at where to go from here, considering our limitations and what's needed to create change.

This book is an invitation, and one you need to be ready for. You must be ready to think differently and you must be ready to be called to a higher standard of leadership where you become the architect of your wellbeing-centred educational institution. You must be ready to take brave, bold action, and to recognise the power and autonomy you have in your school setting – which, I can share with you, is far more than you possibly realise. You must be ready to question everything, from systems and process to beliefs and assumptions. You must be ready to dive deep into the work of wellbeing, to take action, to try new things, and to go against the grain at times. This book isn't just about the work of wellbeing, it's about the revolution our schools need to undertake to support our educators – and that you, as a leader, need to champion.

There are three things I'd like you to reflect on as you work your way through the chapters that lie ahead:

1. What kind of leader are you, and what kind of leader do you want to be?
2. What kind of school are you designing, building and working in each day?
3. What kind of school do you dream and desire to work in?

Let's get started.

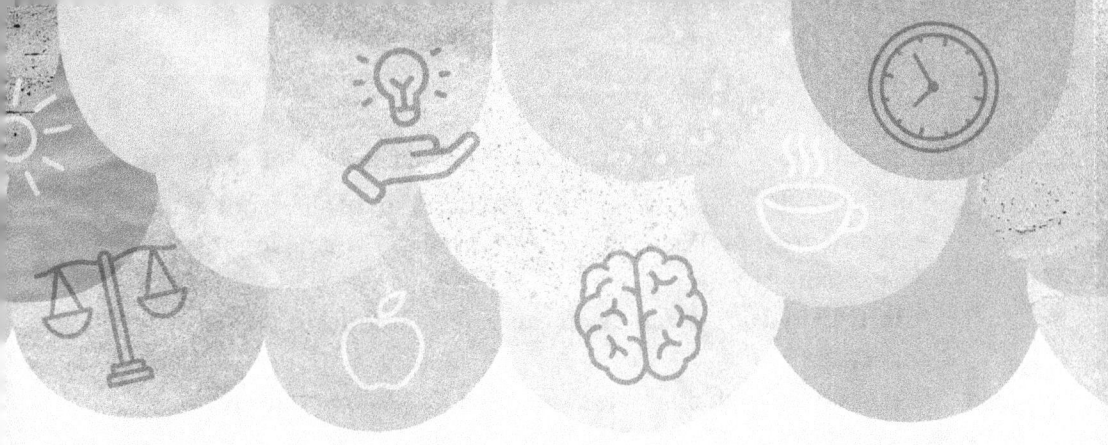

Part 1

The Why of Wellbeing Leadership

To create a wellbeing-centred workplace we must consider five factors:
1. **Purpose:** Why should wellbeing be at the heart of all we do?
2. **Past and present:** What can we learn from the past, to improve the present?
3. **Priority:** How do we make staff wellbeing a priority through our actions?
4. **Perspective:** What do we need to understand about ourselves as leaders?
5. **People:** Who are the people in our workplace and what does each of them bring?

These five factors help us to understand what we are doing, why it matters, what we need to know about ourselves, and how wellbeing leadership can expand our impact. They also let us acknowledge the past with compassion, learn lessons from it and use those learnings to influence the present and future.

Up until now, no leadership approach has been quite as explicit in regards to considering staff wellbeing. Instead of being driven by what is best for students, we now need to consider things such as workload, psychological safety, stress thresholds, and our staff's physical, mental and emotional health and wellbeing when we implement new initiatives, make changes to curriculum or adjust how our daily timetable operates. Every single thing should now be considered through a staff wellbeing lens: *Do staff have capacity for this? Do they have the time and space needed to learn before implementation? Do they have the resources they need to do this well?*

In order for wellbeing to be top of mind in our leadership, we need to not only approach it with logic, pragmatism and systemisation, but with deep self-awareness and compassion. We must recognise the impact our leadership has on staff wellbeing, not just for others but for ourselves, too.

Wellbeing leadership truly is a combination of head and heart work; this is something I know from experience. My journey is one that required (and still does) plenty of personal development and deep self-awareness. In my first book, *Teacher Wellbeing: A Real Conversation for Teachers and Leaders*, I shared with you my own journey of exhaustion, chronic stress and imminent burnout. Even though I wrote that book almost four years after first entering my GP's office to ask for help, I really didn't process the magnitude of what had happened until I put those words on paper.

These days, having now told my story countless times and reflected on my growth, I have a deep understanding of how my personal wellbeing affects my day-to-day life, *and* how it influences who I am as an educator, colleague and leader. I have transformed my own wellbeing, as well as how I believe wellbeing needs to be considered by leaders.

While wellbeing is now something I preach as needing to be front of mind for leaders and educators, I haven't always operated from this space. In fact, I haven't always believed what I believe now. That's the beautiful thing about being human, though: we are malleable, adaptable and can change. We can rethink and redesign our beliefs and values, altering the way we make decisions and behave.

To do this we require high levels of self-awareness, along with discipline, openness and willingness: discipline to do the work, openness to explore how things could be different, and willingness to change. Then we need to let go of everything that existed before and be ready for what's new.

When I reflect on my own wellbeing and how I showed up at work, be it when I was teaching, or in leadership, there were so many things that impacted my ability to work and lead well. When I think about who I was then, how I worked, what my priorities were and the tasks I deemed important, my own and others' wellbeing was not a factor I considered. Instead, I was intently focused on what needed to be done, driven by transactions and making things happen, regardless of how I or anyone else felt. I didn't realise I needed connection, compassion or patience; and while I cared for others, I didn't see the value in prioritising their wellbeing over getting things done. Work came first. At the time, I had no idea that the way I was being, the decisions I made as a leader and how I worked with the teams I led was impacting my colleagues' wellbeing. It is fair to say I had very little, if any, self-awareness and that I was not leading with wellbeing in mind.

Self-awareness really is the key to workplace wellbeing. We think wellbeing is about morning teas and yoga, but the first step is actually self-awareness.

In the last few years, I have run numerous professional development (PD) sessions for educators and workplaces on building self-awareness through the lens of wellbeing, focusing on how to cultivate energy to function well, build healthy resilience strategies, and develop the capacity to understand and regulate emotions as adults. These sessions have been described to me by participants as essential to wellbeing and something every adult should do. Many participants identify that without self-awareness we can't change ourselves, support others or improve workplaces.

Self-awareness is what allows us to drive change, seek solutions and find new ideas. Most importantly, self-awareness supports us to have compassion for ourselves and others, build positive connections and understand how our daily habits impact how we show up to work. It helps us realise that our physical, mental and emotional health is the foundation of everything.

Over time I have shifted from an ego-driven teacher and leader wanting it to be my way to someone who recognises there is no right way. Through cultivating self-awareness, what I know to be most powerful in our schools is the need to come together to create thriving workplaces for ourselves and others. Doing this does not require us to leave our personal lives at the door, but instead appreciate, connect with and value each individual and what they bring with them. We must realise that it is the individuals who make the collective, and the collective that makes the culture of our workplaces.

As we step into knowing that we as leaders must consider, address and lead staff wellbeing, we have to acknowledge that this requires a shift in the why, how and what of leadership as we know it.

Never before have we been asked to explicitly consider the wellbeing of staff in decision-making, new initiatives or changes we make in regard to student learning or pedagogy. However, if we are to consciously consider staff wellbeing as a major consideration in change processes and decision-making, we must be ready for a new phase of leadership – one that puts staff wellbeing at the centre of all we do (not just students).

Each of the chapters that makes up part 1 is designed to help you explore and consider this new phase of leadership. Most importantly, it is about recognising that wellbeing leadership is about how we lead our workplace, not about what we do for other people's wellbeing.

As President of Columbia University, Minouche Shafik so accurately said, 'In the past jobs were about muscles, now they're about brains, but in future they'll be about the heart.' This too reflects the new phase of leadership we as educational leaders are now entering. This is the revolution. This is what it means to lead with staff wellbeing at the centre.

Chapter 1

Purpose

Why Wellbeing Leadership Matters

As leaders in schools, we are often told that our number one priority should be our students. This makes sense: students are the reason we are there, the reason schools exist, the reason teachers teach, and the reason we come together to make schools great places. However, students are not our only responsibility as leaders.

When we consider leadership through the lens of staff wellbeing, we see that our role is also to create and cultivate an environment that allows staff to feel well, work well, team well and lead well. This is what wellbeing leadership is all about. When we do this, we not only make decisions that are right for our students, but we also make decisions that are right for our staff. When we're making changes we consider what both students and staff need, and we prioritise what is important for both students and staff.

Understanding that the purpose of wellbeing leadership is to create a school where everyone can thrive shifts our perspective. It is not just about the students; it is about the people who teach them, too. This is why wellbeing leadership matters.

What is wellbeing?

There are multiple definitions, frameworks and ways to define wellbeing. As great as it is that there is so much thought leadership devoted to wellbeing, this can also be quite hindering to the work we are trying to do. How can we improve or address something if we don't know or all agree what it is?

I have stood in front of 200-plus people and asked them to share what wellbeing is to them: what it looks like personally and professionally, and what they do to improve or maintain their wellbeing. While there are similarities across the room, no two answers are ever the same.

There is a direct correlation between daily tasks and staff wellbeing, yet this is not always clear or well understood. Wellbeing is as much about how we tackle our inbox and the procedures and expectations for reporting and planning as it is about the energy our staff permeate. It's about how we get through our to-do list, collaborate and function as cohesive teams, show up to staff meetings, contribute to the school vision, engage with change and commit to our work – not just in our classrooms or offices but across the school community. Wellbeing is influenced by every action we take, conversation we have and decision we make. This is why wellbeing needs to be at the centre of every school-improvement agenda, strategic plan and school vision (see figure 1).

When I think about my own wellbeing journey, there are many contributing factors I now understand to be imperative – and they are not things such as massages, mani-pedis or morning teas. For me, wellbeing exists around my ability to regulate my emotions, including understanding them, finding meaning in them, reflecting on them, and strengthening my self-awareness. It is taking into account the different elements of energy and function, which involves things such as sleep, nutrition and physical activity, and engaging in non-negotiables within these areas each day. Additionally, I have built a suite of healthy resilience strategies (meditation, time in nature, rest, therapy), which equip me to handle life's challenges – because, let's be honest, no matter how much you work on your wellbeing, the ups and downs of life are inevitable.

These components – regulating emotions, building resilience and maintaining energy levels – form the foundation of my personal wellbeing.

These are the things that help me to be well. However, it's important to note that this is my personal approach to wellbeing, and I have worked tirelessly to be able to develop these internal resources. And, when we look at creating a workplace that prioritises wellbeing, we need to consider more than just individual factors.

Figure 1: Workplace wellbeing and culture

In my previous book, *Teacher Wellbeing*, I shared a multitude of wellbeing definitions, including one from the World Health Organization (2022) which focuses on mental health as a state of wellbeing:

> Mental health is a state of well-being in which an individual realizes his or her own abilities, can cope with the normal stresses of life, can work productively and is able to make a contribution to his or her community.

While there are many definitions, let me show you why this one is key to considering how we look at staff and educator wellbeing. In table 1, I break the WHO definition into its four key parts, and explain how each can be interpreted to support wellbeing and how we work.

Purpose 13

Table 1: Breaking down the WHO definition of wellbeing

Key part of WHO definition	What this means for us	How we can use this	Questions to ask
An individual realises his or her own abilities.	This highlights the importance of knowing and utilising our strengths.	Strengths are activities or actions that we are good at and that energise us, thereby increasing our wellbeing. We can prioritise these in our day-to-day work.	Do I consider my own and my staff members' strengths when allocating work tasks? Do I find ways to work to my strengths? Do I encourage my staff to consider and use their strengths as much as possible?
An individual can cope with the normal stresses of life.	There are normal stresses in life and work. When our wellbeing is higher we are better equipped to cope with these.	Identifying normal, stressful periods in our workplace, such as report-writing or the start of a school year, can help us plan and prepare.	What is normal stress at our school? How can we work to support people during stressful periods? Is this something we need to do individually, collectively or both?
An individual can work productively.	Productivity and wellbeing go hand-in-hand. When wellbeing is high, so too is productivity.	Productivity is not about working fast but working efficiently, effectively and with ease.	Is how I/we work: • efficient (tasks take a reasonable amount of time)? • effective (tasks serve a known and meaningful purpose)? • easeful (the workload is energetically sustainable)?
An individual is able to make a contribution to his or her community.	When wellbeing is high, so too is one's desire to contribute to and be part of their team and wider community.	Contribution in the workplace links to engagement and connecting beyond the classroom.	Am I contributing to and engaging with my team? Do I actively support all colleagues? If not, what is stopping me from contributing and engaging?

In *Teacher Wellbeing*, I also shared with you a framework I developed to bring a structured view to how personal and workplace wellbeing influence teacher wellbeing, based on research and evidence. Not only does this approach ensure the science makes sense for our setting, but it also gives us a tangible and pragmatic way of looking at staff wellbeing (you may also notice the clear links between this approach and the WHO definition). See figure 2.

Figure 2: Staff wellbeing

This a great starting point; however, to take it to the next level, where staff wellbeing is at the centre of decision-making, drives organisational change and improves culture, we need to go even further. We need to not only focus on the wellbeing of individual staff, but consider how we create and maintain a wellbeing-centred workplace.

Defining a wellbeing-centred workplace

A wellbeing-centred workplace has staff wellbeing on every school-improvement agenda. Wellbeing should be part of how and who we are as a workplace. This can't be achieved with an activity-based approach; instead, wellbeing must be at the centre of all thinking and decision-making.

Historically, student outcomes have been the key driver of school improvement. But what if we looked at this differently? What if we put staff wellbeing at the centre of improvement agendas? What if staff wellbeing drove decision-making, and student outcomes were the by-product?

What if, instead of asking, 'How will this benefit students?', we started asking questions that consider staff wellbeing?

> *How will this impact educator wellbeing?*
>
> *Do our educators have the time, energy and capacity for this?*
>
> *What do staff need to be able to maintain energy, productivity and performance when tackling this task?*

I am aware that this may sound like a new way of thinking, and perhaps like a good idea in theory that doesn't seem possible in reality. However, if we are truly wanting to change the landscape for educators, we have to be prepared to think differently, look for original ideas and try new things. This does not mean we disregard the importance of our students, or neglect to consider what they need. But we must understand why prioritising staff wellbeing matters, and how it impacts student learning and the school environment.

Just some of the many benefits of prioritising staff wellbeing include:

- **Improved personal wellbeing and self-efficacy:** Each staff member understands what wellbeing means to them and how it impacts their life both in and out of the workplace. They have the confidence to proactively select and implement strategies.
- **Improved collective wellbeing and collective efficacy:** Collectively, staff have a shared definition of wellbeing and use a common language. They reflect on current ways of working, know how to support each other and collaborate to find solutions, feeling confident to make a difference.
- **Enhanced school culture:** Staff wellbeing is valued and a key driver in decision-making. It is openly discussed with systems, structures and processes put in place to support personal and workplace wellbeing.
- **Improved student learning and student outcomes:** Staff are more aware of students' academic, social and emotional needs, helping them to foster better relationships. They are more organised,

well-planned and present, allowing them to be more open to change and improvement.

Embracing opportunity

Openness to new ideas is essential in a wellbeing-centred workplace, however, looking for new ideas is not always our default. In his book *Originals: How Non-Conformists Move the World*, organisational psychologist Adam Grant uses a term I think is imperative to the change work we need to do in schools right now. That term is 'vuja de'. No doubt you are familiar with the term 'deja vu' – that feeling that you have experienced something before, even though it is a brand-new situation. Well, according to Grant (2017), vuja de occurs when we face something familiar, but we see it with a fresh perspective that enables us to gain new insights into old problems. Right now, more than ever we need vuja-de. We need a fresh perspective and new insights for old problems we continue to face. I think we can all agree that teachers are overworked and time-poor with increased workloads, and that there are many job vacancies in education across the country because of this. This isn't a new problem. These are things we all know, things we have all spoken about and things that we know matter. However, It's time to look at these familiar problems in a different way so we can start to gain new awareness and ideas to solve them.

In education, many of us want to hold on to how things used to be – when we first started teaching, before Covid, in the 'good old days'. The problem is, this is no longer our reality. Nostalgia for what was inhibits us from innovating, from letting go, from removing our own ego and the need to be right, comfortable and certain. We need to stop letting nostalgia influence us. Instead, we must be brave enough to embrace the concept of vuja de, and see these current issues as opportunities to evolve, innovate and revolutionise education and schools. Embracing these opportunities will allow us to create workplaces that put staff wellbeing first, and that are aligned with current evidence-based approaches to workplace design. It's how we will create workplaces that are desirable and attractive to the future teachers we need to have walk through our door and to ensure we retain the wonderful teachers we currently have.

If we know this (and I think many of us do), why is it so hard to do things differently? Why haven't we moved past collecting data? Why haven't we taken action?

Why haven't we embraced Peter DeWitt's work on de-implementation (2022) and started proactively removing, reducing or replacing ineffective practices?

Why haven't we looked to make small changes in each school when we so easily can?

Why haven't we made things such as pay, term breaks and what a teacher is expected to do beyond the classroom uniform across the country?

How bad do we need to let it get before we take drastic action?

Doing things differently means letting go of the old and being ready to run with the new. For many, this feels a little scary and overwhelming, and I can't blame you if you feel this way. While we are on the edge of a new way of working and operating, there is still so much we don't know. Being in this space, which I call the transition space, is hard. We aren't where we used to be, yet we aren't where we want to be, either. It is an uncomfortable place to be and, right now, transition is happening in so many different ways.

Many of us are part of what I call the 'transition generation'. The nine-to-five, live-to-work mindset that began in the industrial revolution has been passed down to us. We have seen those before us dedicate themselves to their job, missing out on opportunities to make memories with family and friends, waiting until they retire to take that trip or start that hobby, with many realising it's too late and never getting that chance. We're seeing younger colleagues, friends and family entering the workforce and asking questions like 'What's this about?' or declaring 'I am not doing that.' We've seen quiet quitting and job hopping become normal. No longer do young people expect to go to university and have one job or even career for their entire life. For those of us who sit in the middle of these spaces, this can feel icky. We are torn between 'the old way' and 'the new way'. The new way includes flexible working hours, four-day weeks, a more focused work approach, an emphasis on emotional intelligence in the workplace, and a shift to focus on staff wellbeing and mental health over profit outcomes and performance. This is in fact the reality of the workplace now. If we want to continue to attract and keep great educators we have to recognise that, yes, there is a transition we can't ignore – but it is also an exciting time to start redesigning and recreating how our schools operate and function.

The need for purposeful change

With so much discussion around staff and educator wellbeing, and the need to attract and retain more educators, we need to think differently, make changes, and act fast. We no longer have time to wait.

We have collected lots of data, declaring that teaching is overwhelming, stressful and causes burnout, and are counting the number of teachers needed to get us out of the teacher shortage. It seems we are putting a lot of time and energy into this data collection, which is not only draining but, to be honest, depressing. Focusing on what's wrong with education requires a lot of energy, which doesn't leave much, if any, space to consider what is great, what opportunities we have, how we can change or what we could innovate. We only have a certain amount of energy and cognitive capacity each day; if we use it to focus on the problem, that doesn't leave much room for solutions – and right now, we need solutions.

In my first book, *Teacher Wellbeing*, I shared with you my own journey and experience of occupational stress and being very close to burnout. I provided some clear examples of what wellbeing is, some new ways for thinking about wellbeing with an emphasis on individual wellbeing strategies (energy and function, resilience and emotional regulation), and workplace wellbeing (engagement, productivity and performance and growth). I provided practical strategies for individuals and schools to implement, which I have outlined in table 2.

(These are unpacked in detail in *Teacher Wellbeing: A Real Conversation for Teachers and Leaders*.)

Table 2: Practical strategies for teachers and schools

What can I do? *Practical strategies for teachers*	What can we do? *Practical strategies for schools*
Build positive emotions Take responsibility Practise self-compassion Set boundaries Create sustainable habits	Build positive relationships Set a clear vision with supportive goals Utilise staff strengths Have strong infrastructure Foster flexibility

While these strategies are a great starting point, it is now time to expand on these.

The truth is, we can implement as many strategies as we like. But unless we have well-considered, well-planned, intentional long-term strategic approaches to change at individual, team and workplace levels, along with how we are working (systems and structures, daily organisation and planning approaches), we run the risk of applying band-aid strategies that address symptoms rather than the cause. And, to be honest, that is not good enough. We need to be willing to dig a little deeper, to go beneath the surface, to get our hands dirty and do the real work of wellbeing leadership. This is what's required to address the problems, shift the culture of our schools and improve how we feel, work, team and lead.

If we don't flip the script and think differently, we run the risk of doing what we have always done; and isn't doing the same thing over and over again and expecting a different result what some refer to as the definition of insanity?

Right now, we are doing lots of what we have always done:
- Hiring more teachers to work in schools that are structured and organised the same way.
- Teaching the same curriculum (there is a new version, but it is still largely the same).
- Implementing new programs, but not training all staff in how to effectively and properly run them.
- Working the same hours in the same ways.
- Implementing wellbeing solutions based on activities at an individual level rather than addressing the core issues.
- Having a reactive rather than preventative approach (in all areas – not just exclusive to staff wellbeing).
- Expecting all educators to plan, work and do the same things because 'equitable' means focusing on tasks and time.
- Seeing productivity in terms of time rather than output.
- Organising timetables without any thought to how staff best work.
- Having too many priorities and no clear vision.
- Starting all new school initiatives in January, overwhelming staff.
- Not being transparent about decision-making, letting the gossip take over.

- Being unclear about what 'finished' looks like, so educators know they can stop working and go home.
- Having multiple ways of doing the same thing.
- Making a decision because 'it's good for the students' without any consideration of staff capacity for quality implementation.

I could go on, and I'm sure you could add plenty to this list, too. The point I am making is that for things to be different, we need to do things differently. It's time to have some fun, dream a little, and explore some innovative ways in which we could redesign our schools. It's time to consider all the possibilities, no matter how crazy they seem. This is where we innovate, create and revolutionise.

In the list below, I have offered ideas from 'dream lists' educators have shared with me, and I have added some of my own. It's exciting to see that some of these ideas are already happening in some schools. Others I have added simply because if you can't dream it, you can't do it – and right now, more than ever, it is time to dream.

Can we:
- Have four-day weeks (for staff, students or both)?
- Utilise external coaches and experts to support student learning, finding more space for educators to connect and collaborate?
- Allocate work based on strengths, not equitable distribution of tasks?
- Agree time on task and productivity are not the same?
- Offer opportunities to work flexibly? (For example, can a team meet at 7am instead of 3pm? If an educator is not required to teach a lesson until 10am, can they arrive on site a little later than usual?)
- Include more online learning opportunities for students via experts to support educators in teaching subjects that are not their specialty?
- Have real, meaningful discussions to drive real, meaningful change and that focus on the cause, not the symptom?
- Organise timetables and daily schedules to support when people work best? (This is known as job crafting.)
- Introduce new initiatives in a staggered fashion rather than all at once, in January?
- Focus on de-implementation rather than implementation?
- Consider staff capacity and resources (time and energy) before starting something new?

- Cycle units of work and assessment across terms rather than all starting and ending at the same time?
- Redistribute workload to reduce the intensity of each term?

In my ideal redesign of education, we would work (and be paid for) 48 weeks a year like all other professions. This would give us approximately eight weeks to redistribute the workload that makes term time so intense. Students would still have two weeks' holiday, but these would become term breaks for educators where we would spend the first week on designated tasks, such as report-writing, parent teacher meetings, planning, marking, PD, open nights, presentation evenings and getting ready for the term ahead. The second week would be an opportunity to rest, switch off, and work if desired but from home or a place of choice. This would mean, instead of intense terms, which impact stress levels and wellbeing, we redistribute workload to term breaks, meaning during term time all we do is teach and focus on student learning. This may be an unpopular opinion, however term intensity is something many agree is unsustainable. This is a possible solution, and one that could be significantly impactful for staff wellbeing.

For some of you, these ideas may seem far off or even impossible. But why is that? Is it because we *think* they're impossible? Because it seems like too much work? Because we are already too busy? Because we think we can't?

Until we have evidence that something can't or won't work (because of policy out of our control, or because it doesn't work in our setting), we need to be open, curious and willing to explore new ideas and ways of working, leading and operating as a school. This is the only way we are going to lead with staff wellbeing in mind, innovate, let go of the past, and revolutionise schools to be great workplaces.

We may not know if these things are possible, but we need to be willing to try. We need to decide if we want to give it a go, and be prepared to succeed or learn from what didn't work.

So, are you ready? Are you ready to ask better questions, to dream, to try, to at times fail and other times succeed? To take risks, innovate and lead the revolution? I hope so.

Creating a culture of wellbeing

A wellbeing-centred workplace doesn't happen by chance. It happens through intentional action and decision-making, based on shared beliefs and values, with increased awareness of who we are and with individual and collective responsibility. Most importantly, however, it requires a culture of wellbeing.

A culture of wellbeing relies on us knowing the fundamentals that shape how we work and function. By establishing and living this culture day to day, we work within consistent, shared beliefs and values that shape not only what we do, but who we are as an organisation. This draws upon collective efficacy and collective responsibility. A culture of wellbeing is one in which:

- we understand, value and appreciate our staff
- we interact intentionally and mindfully with one another
- we make decisions based on what is good for staff and what supports their wellbeing
- we can have robust, open dialogue and brave, vulnerable conversations.

There are four key elements that make up a wellbeing-centred workplace (see table 3 overleaf). Considering these elements allows us to understand all the moving parts: the what, why and how of our organisation. Each of these areas connects with and contributes to a culture of wellbeing in its own way.

Creating a culture of wellbeing requires more than just morning teas and yoga classes. It is more than being happy all the time, thinking of things each day you are grateful for or engaging in sporadic meditation. In fact, recent research surveying 46,336 workers in 233 organisations found no evidence that suggested individual-level mental wellbeing interventions such as mindfulness, resilience and stress management, relaxation classes or wellbeing apps benefit staff. Rather, organisational interventions – such as changes to scheduling, management practices, staff resources, performance reviews, or job design – may be more beneficial for improving wellbeing in the workplace (Fleming, 2024).

Table 3: Elements of a wellbeing-centred workplace

Feel well	Work well	Team well	Lead well
Feeling well is the sense of feeling positive in the workplace. It is connected to our personal wellbeing, emotional health, connection and belonging, and individual and collective resilience. (Note: feeling well does not mean being happy all the time.)	*Working well* relies on us designing how we work to support staff wellbeing. It involves asking one key question over and over again: 'Does how we work support staff wellbeing?' This is an opportunity to reimagine the systems, structures and processes that inform how we work.	*Teaming well* is often under-estimated or not even considered in discussions around staff wellbeing. It's about how our teams are designed, how they're connected, how they function, and how they create collective support for wellbeing.	*Leading well* is a key driver in creating and maintaining a wellbeing-centred workplace. Leaders play a crucial role in improving staff wellbeing. Leading well means a leader takes care of their own wellbeing while also supporting others to do so.

Individual wellbeing activities alone are not enough to create a culture of wellbeing and a wellbeing-centred workplace. There are many moving parts, complexities and pieces of the puzzle to take into account. We have to be prepared to do these things as well as reflect on and improve who we are as a collective. We have to be curious and open-minded to allow for new ways of doing things. We have to embrace vuja de. We have to say yes when we are used to saying no, or no when we are used to saying yes. More importantly, we need to stop pulling educators out of the stream, and instead start asking why they are falling in to begin with. This is how we address the cause rather than the symptoms.

As a leader, you may feel overwhelmed or out of your depth when you're considering this, and that's okay. Perhaps it's to be expected: we don't know what is coming, but we do know it will be different. The old ways of education, schools and being a teacher no longer exist so, whether we are ready or not, we must create something new.

We're in transition, moving away from how it used to be to a place that is brand new, unknown and unimaginable, but undoubtedly one we will all benefit from.

Personally, I feel like the best is yet to come.

Collective beliefs and attributes

Beliefs play an integral role in our ability to influence workplace wellbeing. It's our beliefs that shape our existence, the stories we tell ourselves and the meaning we make. They can hinder or help us to grow and change. We need to be aware of this for ourselves, as well as for our teams and workplaces, and consider the differing beliefs that might be causing tension or challenge.

The following six beliefs create a foundation from which we can centre staff wellbeing at the core of our workplaces and school culture. These beliefs need to be internalised not just by leaders, but by all staff.

The six core beliefs:

1. **Staff wellbeing matters because staff matter (not just because it improves student outcomes).** Staff matter. They are the worker bees, the drivers, the ones who keep schools moving. To focus on staff wellbeing only because it improves student outcomes dilutes the value and impact. We can try to implement new teaching and learning initiatives, send staff to PD or have our leaders drive change, but the truth is, if staff wellbeing and culture isn't optimal, nothing we implement will have its desired effect. We also need to acknowledge that our educators and staff in our school are people first. They have lives, interests, and needs beyond the workplace. This matters, too, not just the work they do inside our schools.
2. **Everyone is responsible for the work of wellbeing.** Each person has a role to play. We also need to embrace that each of us is equally responsible for the change we make in this space. We all need to collectively take action for ourselves and also for each other. As leaders this means we need to empower staff, not just rescue them, equipping them to support their own wellbeing in and out of the workplace. And, as leaders, we need to ensure this thinking applies

to us, too. We can't look to our principal as middle leaders, or the system as principals, we need to band together and do what we can.
3. **Our personal wellbeing impacts our professional wellbeing.** We need to understand that our (and our staff members') personal wellbeing dramatically impacts workplace wellbeing. Sleep, nutrition, movement, rest, mindfulness, emotional regulation, resilience and coping strategies, the people we spend time with, our internal thoughts and building positive emotions – all of this impacts wellbeing at work. As leaders we can't tell people what time to go to bed or what to eat, nor are we responsible for making sure staff exercise or move their body, but we do need to ensure we offer staff education, support and resources in this area. Further to this is the need to be aware of and open to hearing when workload or expectations may be impacting these things. For example, if a school musical goes late into the evening and staff are expected to be at work at 8am the next morning, we need to be aware that this will impact sleep, and is something we might need to address.
4. **High workplace wellbeing leads to positive school cultures.** If we focus on building aspects of workplace wellbeing such as productivity, engagement, performance and growth and the areas of how we feel, work, team and lead well as outlined in this book, an improved culture is the result. If we only focus on culture, we miss key areas of wellbeing that each individual needs to have to be able to contribute to the team and collective culture of their workplace.
5. **Collective self-awareness drives change.** If we are truly wanting to change ourselves, our teams and our schools, we must understand that self-awareness is key. Self-awareness is not just limited to the individual, but also includes the team and organisation. How do we build self-awareness collectively? How do we pause, reflect and be curious about our behaviours individually and as a team? This is what it takes to become collectively self-aware. When we are collectively self-aware we have the innate ability to question what we do and why we do it. We learn from, critique and analyse our decisions, actions and behaviours through a lens of wellbeing.
6. **Our beliefs are not set; we can modify, change or let go of them.** It's vital to understand the beliefs within our teams and the

larger school context. Through knowing our beliefs we can better understand who we are, and reflect on our choices and where we spend our energy. Many of us bypass the time needed to reflect on our beliefs, instead taking them as fact or not knowing they are there. Additionally, we need to understand that we can modify, change or let go of our beliefs.

The change we seek isn't going to happen by chance, wishing, waiting or hoping. We must collectively be ready and willing to cultivate and draw upon the following six attributes:

1. **Bravery:** This is going to take bravery like never before. We need to be brave enough to try new things, take risks and make changes in areas that haven't changed in a long time (if ever). We need to be prepared to fail.
2. **Boldness:** We need boldness to call out those around us, to call out what we have always done that no longer serves up, and to suggest new, out-of-the-box ideas.
3. **Courage:** We need courage to suggest new ideas and to go against the grain, to do something for the first time and be okay with not knowing what is going to happen, and to say yes when everyone else is saying no, or no when everyone else is saying yes.
4. **Vulnerability:** We need vulnerability to speak up, to say what others are thinking but not brave enough to say, to discuss things that we have avoided or skirted around in the past, and to bare all as we go all in for the change we need.
5. **Compassion:** We need compassion for ourselves and others as we navigate this change process.
6. **Grit:** There is no denying it: this won't be easy. There will be times when you don't know where to go or what to do, and you will want to give up. Grit is what allows us to get our hands dirty and face obstacles head-on; it's what will get you through when challenges arise.

These six attributes are not just essential for you as a leader, but to cultivate across your staff community. These skills can feel uncomfortable, often requiring us to utilise parts within us that have not always been defined as true leadership skills. However, these attributes are essential. We can't create a psychologically safe workplace without ensuring we, and our staff, can be vulnerable, brave and courageous, openly sharing what's on our minds without fear of being ridiculed or judged.

Cultivating these attributes will allow you to safely step into a space of change, knowing it will be hard, icky and at times confronting, but oh so worth it. With these skills, we can rethink and redesign schools to make them the wellbeing-centred workplaces we need them to be.

Chapter summary

- We are entering a new phase of leadership – one that requires us to see the support of staff wellbeing as a necessary factor in doing our job well.
- A wellbeing-centred workplace considers staff capacity, space, time and energy when making decisions and taking action.
- Wellbeing includes how we feel, work, team and lead; it is not solely about activities, social gatherings or reacting to staff moods.
- We need to embrace vuja de – to think differently about the same problem we continue to face.
- The only way to create change is to take daring risks, to be brave, courageous and vulnerable, and to be open and ready for change instead of resisting it.

From theory to action

What is wellbeing?

Let's revisit the questions from earlier in the chapter that relate to the WHO definition of wellbeing. Consider each question and answer them based on your current ways of working. Use the 'actions I could take' column to identify one or two small actions you could implement for each area.

Key part of WHO definition	Questions to ask	Actions I could take
An individual realises his or her own abilities.	Do I consider my own and my staff members' strengths when allocating work tasks? Do I find ways to work to my strengths? Do I encourage my staff to consider and use their strengths as much as possible?	
An individual can cope with the normal stresses of life.	What is normal stress at our school? How can we work to support people during stressful periods? Is this something we need to do individually, collectively or both?	
An individual can work productively.	Is how I/we work: - efficient (tasks take a reasonable amount of time)? - effective (tasks serve a known and meaningful purpose)? - easeful (the workload is energetically sustainable)?	
An individual is able to make a contribution to his or her community.	Am I contributing to and engaging with my team? Do I actively support all colleagues? If not, what is stopping me from contributing and engaging?	

Time to try some vuja de

With a huge section of this chapter asking you to dream, play and rethink your school's approach to supporting staff wellbeing, consider these questions (you may even like to take these to your team, wellbeing committee or wider staff):

- What ideas, dreams or opportunities do you think might be possible or worth exploring?
- What areas of your school need to be revolutionised?
- Where can some quick changes be made?
- What feelings and emotions do you need to embrace to allow for these things to happen?
- What might get in the way of these things happening?
- If you could only choose one thing to change right now, what would you choose and why?

Chapter 2

Past and Present

Learning from our Mistakes

By far the most popular chapter of my first book, *Teacher Wellbeing*, was chapter 3: Where We Got it Wrong. In that chapter I outlined ten mistakes we have made in our efforts to address teacher wellbeing. It didn't seem right to write a second book without including a similar chapter. Not because I want to highlight where we have gone wrong, but because mistakes help us learn and grow. We need to recognise, accept and be okay with our mistakes. While these mistakes may be hard to read about, there is truth in all of them. Please know that this chapter isn't designed to induce guilt or attribute blame. I truly believe each of us is doing the best we can with what we have. We have to remember that, historically, we have had very little time, resourcing and support to develop our skills in leading staff wellbeing. We have had to piece together what we could with what we had, and that is okay. This chapter might give you a few aha moments, realisations and prompts to think and do differently – which is a good thing, because right now, that is exactly what we need.

So, with open hearts and minds, being brave, courageous and vulnerable, let's do this.

1. We made all the decisions

As leaders, we often think everything sits with us – but in most cases, including that of staff wellbeing, it doesn't. Leaders everywhere have sat in meeting rooms and around tables, brainstorming what they can do, should do or would like to do for staff wellbeing. Ideas have been suggested, strategies plotted, tasks undertaken and initiatives implemented – all with good intention, yet without asking or collaborating with educators themselves.

It's easy to understand why this happens. As leaders we genuinely care about staff wellbeing, so when we notice our own staff not at their best, or realise that we should perhaps try to do things differently, we go straight into action mode. We want to help, fix and make things better – this is in our leader DNA – yet this action-driven, leader-responsible approach isn't always the most impactful for long-term change.

While in some ways we are responsible for ensuring staff wellbeing is a priority and that it is given the time, budget and focus it needs, we aren't responsible for thinking up all the solutions or doing all the work required to make changes we desire. We also can't be held responsible for how our staff manage their own wellbeing. Even though we may offer numerous resources, PD opportunities, mentoring, coaching and ongoing support, what an individual does with what is available sits with them. Our job is to ensure our staff have the resources to make informed, meaningful and sustainable decisions about what matters most.

What to do instead

To move towards collective responsibility we must collaborate, delegate and empower all staff to do this work with us. This means including all staff in the decision-making process, in reviewing data and having conversations about where to next, in suggesting ideas and implementing different plans, as well as in reviewing and reflecting on what is and isn't working.

We also need to be patient. It is understandable to want things to change as quickly as possible, but to do this process well, we need to give it time. Collaborative planning and implementation may appear to take more time than if all decisions were made in leadership meetings alone, but the impact will be far greater if done together and with the opportunity for staff voice.

2. We relied too much on ad-hoc physical wellbeing initiatives

Yoga classes, morning teas, fruit bowls and a herbal tea selection that would rival any T2 store – this is all too common when it comes to workplace wellbeing initiatives. While these things may be helpful, they only skim the surface of what wellbeing really is and requires.

Physical wellbeing includes things such as nutrition, sleep, movement, rest and hydration. While many workplace wellbeing initiatives start here, they also end here. These initiatives are often sporadic, too – a monthly yoga class, a fruit bowl people seldom choose to eat from (because usually there is chocolate, too), and an occasional 'Biggest Loser' club for those on a weight-loss mission. To truly benefit physical wellbeing, and for the impacts to extend to our mental and emotional wellbeing, we need to build sustainable, daily habits that we persevere with rather than sporadic activities.

What to do instead

It is important to keep an eye on physical wellbeing, as it does contribute significantly to all other areas of wellbeing; however, we must make this explicit. We need to ensure that education occurs in regards to the benefits of these initiatives and all areas of physical wellbeing, and that we let staff choose the strategy that works for them.

Yoga offers significant mental, emotional and cognitive benefits, as can running, playing a team sport or swimming. We know sleep is important, but how well do we understand our sleep hygiene, or the importance of natural light and how this links to our circadian rhythm? Do we know that choosing chocolate over fruit can negatively impact how we function in the afternoon?

The key when focusing on physical wellbeing is not to look at the activity or strategy in isolation, but instead bring everything back to why – energy and function.

3. We didn't upskill ourselves in workplace wellbeing

As we learned in chapter 1, workplace wellbeing is not the same as personal wellbeing – yet many current approaches to workplace wellbeing are centred on personal wellbeing. As leaders, we might find ourselves looking for an external expert who can help build personal strategies for staff, when we also need to look at how we as leaders can build our capacity to address workplace wellbeing. This includes looking at systems, structures and processes, addressing workload and stress factors, and finding ways to increase productivity, engagement and meaningful work.

I appreciate that we need and want to support staff to build their own wellness strategies, because as we know, if individuals aren't doing what they can to support their personal wellbeing, it does make it challenging to benefit from what the workplace is doing. However, we must understand that as leaders we are not responsible for micromanaging our staff members' personal wellbeing. We can give them information and help them learn (this is where personal wellbeing PD sessions are useful), but as individuals they need to take action. This means that we need to shift most of our attention and effort to what we can control and influence: what happens in our workplace.

What to do instead

Stop focusing so much on personal strategies and instead learn how as a leader you can influence and empower staff to drive their own change (this is where implementing coaching is paramount). Importantly, engage in PD opportunities that allow you to develop as a leader of staff wellbeing, and that empower you with tools and strategies to support staff and drive change in your context, rather than just adding more to your plate. Upskill and learn about what you can do for workplace wellbeing, and be brave enough to take action to address things that may be causing stress or low wellbeing, rather than continually focus on the symptoms.

4. We ran ad-hoc PD sessions

A PD session at the start of the year ticks the staff wellbeing box – but does it really make a difference? Ad-hoc and one-off wellbeing sessions have very little impact on overall staff wellbeing and long-term change. Why? Because they tend to focus mostly on physical wellbeing and are sporadic in nature. Ad-hoc staff PD sessions are not the answer to driving meaningful change in your school (be they on staff wellbeing or something else).

Ad-hoc PD sessions can be viewed as tokenistic, with staff deciding to disengage before they even begin. With wellbeing being so complex and unique, as well as linked to beliefs, values and culture, attending one workshop is highly unlikely to achieve drastic change or significant impact.

What to do instead

PD is essential, but it needs to be built into your overall school strategic plan and woven into the school week, term and year. Staff wellbeing should be on meeting agendas frequently, PD opportunities for all staff should be consistent and part of a bigger plan, and any wellbeing PD should connect back to what you as a school desire to create. With a range of PD available, it is easy to get distracted – like eating at a buffet and wanting to taste everything. Instead we need to see PD as a fine-dining experience and value it for its sophisticated silver-service offerings. While there is nothing wrong with a buffet, and they do contain a range of tasty dishes, when put together, they don't mesh so well – no one likes their butter chicken on top of their BBQ ribs. When we have a buffet-style approach to PD, it is difficult for staff to know what to implement, what the priority is and where to focus time and energy.

5. We had too much quantitative data and not enough qualitative data

There are certain questions to ask when it comes to leading staff wellbeing, and they need to be asked in both quantitative and qualitative ways. While surveys are great at providing some data, and can usually be done quickly and easily, they don't always give us the depth of information we need. To really understand what is happening in our workplace we have to be prepared to ask open-ended questions and have deep discussion. While this takes time, and may not be as easy as sending out a survey, it can be a great way to find out what is going on beneath the surface. Qualitative responses are even more powerful when combined with quantitative data. Quantitative data can be interpreted in many different ways, with each person bringing their own narrative to what they see.

What to do instead

We need to first focus on understanding the current landscape of staff wellbeing to get a picture of what is really happening. To do this we want to ask staff these three questions:

1. **What is working well?** We want to find out what is working well so we can amplify this and know which things to keep.
2. **Are there any challenges, issues or areas that affect your ability to work efficiently or effectively?** This gives us a clear representation of what the workplace looks like so we can start to see any patterns or trends that we can improve, including around our systems, structures and processes.
3. **What ideas or suggestions do you have for improvement?** This allows staff to have a say in any changes that may occur, and gives them a chance to offer ideas that leaders may not have considered (I have seen this in practice many times before and it is quite exciting to discover what staff suggest).

These questions are also helpful as they allow us to explore anything we may find within the quantitative data we have collected. When done in discussion format, we can ask additional questions to gather more information, which we can't do when staff complete a survey.

6. We put everyone in the same box

Everyone needs to improve their wellbeing, so everyone must need the same thing, right? Wrong. When we put everyone in the same box we devalue their individual wellbeing needs and desires. Not everyone needs to attend a yoga class or wants a meeting-free week. Not everyone wants to attend morning tea or write down three things they are grateful for. While these strategies and interventions may be great for some, they may not be right for others. When looking at what to do for staff wellbeing we need to keep in mind that not everyone is the same and not everyone benefits from the same approach.

What to do instead

Use the questions listed in mistake 5 to get a clear and thorough picture of what is happening in your school. This will help you design meaningful and targeted interventions for your staff as well as consider what each individual and team needs. You can then look to offer targeted training for different people or teams as well as give people the option to choose from what may be on offer that suits their needs and wants.

7. We rescued rather than empowered

As leaders we can think that it's our job to do all the fixing, but it's not. When someone knocks on the office door and says they don't have enough time, their workload is too heavy or they can't meet an agreed deadline, our job isn't to do the work or give out more time – it's to be curious enough to find out what is really going on and to empower others to make changes in areas they can control. This isn't what always happens, though. Instead, we tend to rescue, do the work or grant more time. There are two problems with this. First, it adds more to our own plate, meaning we are increasing our workload and potentially our stress levels, reducing our ability to work well. Second, we are not empowering staff to make any sort of behaviour change, meaning when the issue arises again the only strategy they will have is to get their leader to rescue them. This is not a sustainable strategy for either party.

What to do instead

Building your confidence in utilising coaching questions is a game changer when it comes to empowering rather than rescuing. Coaching allows you to investigate what is really going on for a staff member and work with them to help them decide on action they can take, rather than what you can do for them. When you engage in this strategy, you are freeing yourself up from doing others' work while allowing them to build their self-efficacy, so when the same or a similar problem arises they have the skills and strategy to support themselves rather than coming to you to be rescued.

8. We treated the symptom, not the cause

Staff were tired, so we cancelled meetings. Staff complained about having too many things on their to-do lists, so we extended deadlines. Staff appeared low in energy, so we brought out the morning teas and extra chocolates. Yes, we are all guilty of doing this, me included. However, when we look for a quick fix we aren't addressing the cause, only the symptom. Being tired is a symptom. Feeling like you have a massive to-do list is a symptom. Being low on energy is a symptom. The challenge is to find out what the cause is and address that instead of always focusing on the symptom. If you can find the cause you can prevent it from reoccurring rather than having to treat the symptom again and again.

What to do instead

As a leader, you need to be curious rather than reactionary. You need to respond to symptoms by finding out what's really going, so you can treat the cause rather than apply another band-aid. Report-writing time is a great time to practise this. There is no amount of chocolate frogs that can fix how tired all educators feel around report-writing time, nor should we accept the pressure of this time as normal, seeing it as a phase to simply get through. Instead, we should be reviewing our report-writing timeline, pre-empting this time of normal stress, being curious about how staff are using the time they have, and seeing if there is anything we can change so that the normal stress does not expand into long-term, unmanageable stress.

9. We signed up for the app, survey and pulse check but didn't make good use of it

Staff wellbeing surveys and pulse checks, apps and online questionnaires – they all look like great things to have, but how impactful are they? Data is only as powerful as the change it drives. We can have multiple data sets, graphs, charts and numbers, but unless we do something about those numbers, why bother collecting them in the first place? We need to consider whether the data we are collecting is valuable and meaningful, as well as whether it's the right piece of data for us. There is no point collecting data on staff workload or stress if you don't plan to reduce it. There is no point collecting data on emotional states or resilience strategies if you don't plan to offer PD on how to manage emotions and engage in healthy resilience strategies. Whatever data you collect, you need to be prepared to address what you discover.

What to do instead

First, we need to be discerning about the data we choose to collect. We need to know what we want to find out and consider several tools before selecting one. Choosing one because it appears in your inbox and looks good is not reason enough. To make the data we collect valuable, we need to be curious and use the questions from mistake 5 to go beneath the surface.

With a range of options and data tools out there, it is essential that we make well-informed decisions about what to use, and that a planned and scheduled time is set aside to respond to the data so it becomes meaningful and useful.

10. We had too many priorities and tried to do too many things at once

While I appreciate the urge to run with everything and do all the things, this is part of the problem when it comes to addressing staff wellbeing. The art of leading a wellbeing-centred workplace means coming back to what we believe and stand for, and not getting distracted by every little thing we can or think we should do.

As a leader, it is important to rethink and reconsider change, how decisions are made and how to plan for new initiatives. We need to move from student-centred decision-making and combine this with staff-wellbeing-centred decision-making to create schools where we consider how staff feel, work, team and lead. It is also important to take intentional action and be aware of limitations and how to overcome these, as well as finding ways to slow down and rest – the opposite of what we are so used to doing when it comes to change, innovation and continuous improvement.

What to do instead

Instead, we need to focus on what matters, make data-informed decisions and consider what changes we can make that will give us the biggest return on investment for staff wellbeing in the short and long term. This means not always doing the easiest, most appealing or fun thing. Instead, we need to embrace the true work of wellbeing. We have to be better at saying no, choosing some things for now and saving some for later, or not doing something even though we may want to. We have to recognise what we can control and do what we can with the capacity, energy and resources we have, rather than always adding more to our plate. This includes not just our core business of teaching and supporting students, but everything else in between.

Chapter summary

- We have made some mistakes; let's acknowledge and learn from these.
- Pointing the finger, blaming, denying or justifying these mistakes will not help us move forward.
- Everyone, including all leaders, has been doing the best they can with the knowledge, skills and resources they have.
- We need to be brave enough to see what is going on beneath the surface, collect qualitative data and invite and respond to staff voices.
- We need to treat the cause, not the symptom. This is where meaningful, sustainable, strategic change takes place.

From theory to action

Ten mistakes, ten things to reflect on, ten ways to begin to make change.

This task is simple: go back and read each mistake again. Note down your biggest take-away and one thing you could, or would, like to change or implement right now. It could be something practical, an idea you would like to explore or a mindset shift you would like to make.

Leading staff wellbeing mistakes to reflect on

Mistake	Biggest take-away	One thing to change or implement
We made all the decisions		
We relied too much on ad-hoc physical wellbeing initiatives		
We didn't upskill ourselves in workplace wellbeing		
We ran ad-hoc PD sessions		
We had too much quantitative data and not enough qualitative data		
We put everyone in the same box		
We rescued rather than empowered		
We treated the symptom, not the cause		

Mistake	Biggest take-away	One thing to change or implement
We signed up for the app, survey and pulse check but didn't make good use of it		
We had too many priorities and tried to do too many things at once		

Chapter 3

Priority

A Wellbeing-Centred Workplace

Wellbeing is not separate from daily tasks or operations, from staff outcomes or performance, or from how we plan and teach. It is the driver and the core, and the one area in which, if we focus, everything else benefits. Making wellbeing a priority in an ever-increasingly busy workplace can be challenging, but it is essential.

Being an educator is great profession; therefore, we need to ensure our educators have the opportunities, tools and support they need to be great professionals. This means considering staff in decision-making to ensure they are not overwhelmed or have unrealistic job demands or workload pressures due to constant change. It means being intentional with actions so work is meaningful and purposeful, and everyone benefits. It means ensuring staff are supported and structures are in place to allow individuals and groups to rest frequently. It means rejecting the belief that educators rest only on weekends and 'that's what holidays are for'. If you truly want to create a wellbeing-centred workplace as a leader of staff wellbeing you must put staff at the centre of decision-making, be intentional with the actions you take, and make daily, micro-moments of rest a must. This is what is needed to ensure this profession is sustainable, healthy and supportive of those who work in it, including you.

Shifting to a staff-wellbeing-centred decision-making model, as pictured in figure 3, allows us to prioritise our staff and ensure they have energy and capacity for their already extensive workload. It ensures we nurture the nurturers and design our schools to support how staff work. If we don't do this, we will continue to have overworked, overstretched, dysregulated educators focusing on content before connection, and struggling even more to keep up with the work they need to do.

Figure 3: Staff-wellbeing-centred decision-making model

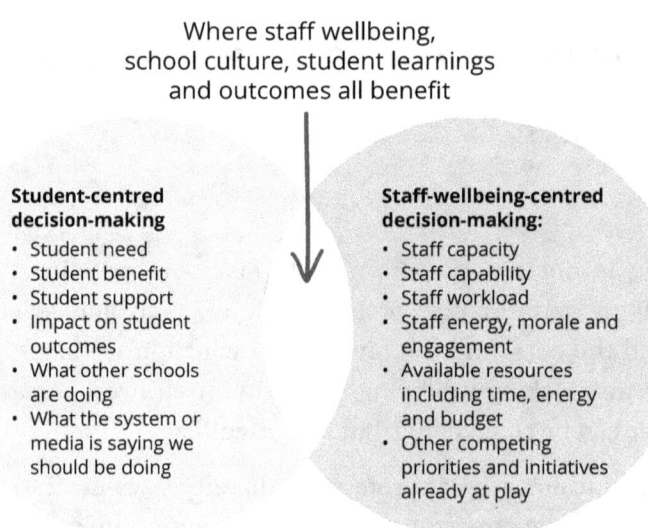

The lack of consideration for staff wellbeing in decision-making is also why we see programs fail, because they aren't carried out in the way that was intended or are quickly replaced by something else. No time is given to asking questions around staff capacity, resources, time and energy or if staff can actually do what's required based on their current way of working. This is wellbeing, and this is culture.

The more we neglect staff wellbeing in decision-making, the more our students are impacted, too, with research showing that the better the wellbeing of an educator, the better they form relationships and teach their students:

> *Teachers who experience lower levels of stress and burnout can create a more conducive learning environment, fostering students' emotional and academic development. (Smith et al., 2019)*

We need to shift from seeing wellbeing as an isolated area to understanding that it must be woven into the fabric of everything we do. I appreciate that, for many, this is a big shift in thinking: it is asking that we no longer see schools as just about students. Until we do this, we will not be sustainably supporting educators to feel, work, team and lead well.

Intentional action

So much of what we focus on in schools is doing. We are constantly and consistently asking ourselves what more we can do. Of course there is a need for action if we want to grow and evolve, but if doing is all we focus on we are missing some key things that can support us to change. This makes it difficult to collectively commit to and engage in sustainable growth as a workplace.

To only focus on doing means we are always adding to our to-do list, our already full plate, our already jam-packed calendar. Focusing on doing alone doesn't allow us to understand why, when or how. It doesn't give us space to consider whether this is really the best thing, whether now is the right time or whether we have capacity to do what we're adding to our list.

When I'm having discussions with leaders and educators about doing less, they commonly respond by saying, 'But our students need it, so we have to do it.' Yes, this may be true, but if teachers don't have the time or capacity to carry an initiative out, to implement it as designed or even learn what they need to before implementation, the desired impact is not going to be achieved.

We often realise this after the fact – as evidenced by the common statement, 'We tried x but it didn't work.' When I explore statements like this with educators, we often uncover that the reason 'x didn't work' was because it was implemented when teachers didn't have the capacity to carry it out because their plate was already full, staff weren't adequately trained so it wasn't implemented as intended, or there wasn't a well-thought-out implementation process. If implementation isn't planned with staff capacity in mind this means the focus goes straight to doing, meaning an educator's need to learn, reflect and plan before doing is missed altogether.

So, if we aren't focusing on doing, what should we focus on instead? The answer is: intentional action (see figure 4).

Figure 4: Intentional action

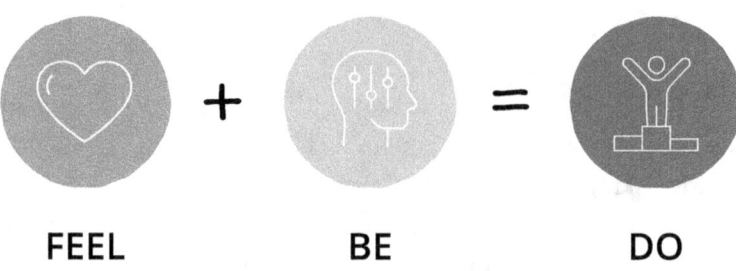

FEEL **BE** **DO**

It is not that we stop doing; instead, there are a few steps to consider before taking action. First, how do we want to feel; and second, who do we want to be.

The concept of Feel + Be = Do is a simple yet powerful framework for facilitating change in schools and promoting a positive culture. Each of the three parts allows us to emphasise the interconnectedness of emotions, behaviours and actions within a work environment, rather than focusing on actions alone. Each component of Feel + Be = Do, when understood and applied, can help us to consider if we should implement something, if we have the capacity to do so, and if we are ready to do so.

Feel

As we are emotional beings, we want to acknowledge this in creating a wellbeing-centred workplace. This applies to undergoing change processes, implementing something new, and considering team and staff collaboration. Emotions play a significant role in the workplace.

People who feel valued, appreciated and emotionally supported are more likely to be engaged and motivated, and experience higher task performance and satisfaction with their work (Fisher, 2002). Conversely, negative emotions such as stress, frustration and anxiety can hinder productivity and wellbeing.

As humans, we are significantly influenced by how we feel and also how we don't want to feel. With this in mind, we need to consider how our staff feel and want to feel when we undertake something new or are approaching a phase of change. As change can impact our identity, sense of belonging and relationships with colleagues, the more we are able to understand and address the mixed emotions of our staff, the more we can sustain and support their motivation and commitment to achieving goals and implementing change (Sikerbol, 2015).

Be

The 'be' component in this equation refers to the behaviours and attitudes demonstrated by staff and teams in the workplace. Behaviours are influenced by our existing culture, leadership and the emotional climate of the workplace.

Behaviour is intentional if we focus on who we want to be after considering how we want to feel. Managing this involves connecting with our values, and reminding ourselves and our staff that who we are being, including our behaviours and actions, is going to reflect the experiences we are having.

Do

With insights into both how we are feeling and who we want to be, we can then use this lens to evaluate any change or growth plan to ensure what we do is achievable, impactful and sustainable.

Feel + Be = Do examples

Let's explore how the Feel + Be = Do formula can be applied when looking to reflect and review classroom culture and student/teacher relationships (see table 4 overleaf).

Table 4: Feel + Be = Do: classroom culture and student/teacher relationships

	Purpose	Current state	Desired state
Feel	To understand how staff are feeling and how they would like to feel.	Teachers feel overwhelmed and stressed because behaviour issues disrupt the learning environment.	Teachers feel empowered and satisfied when managing classroom behaviour.
Be	To observe the behaviours staff are exhibiting and whether these are helpful, sustainable and reflective of the desired culture.	Behaviour management is inconsistent and unclear for both staff and students. A punitive approach is more common.	Teachers are confident, providing clear expectations and using restorative approaches.
Do	To use the above to derive meaningful and purposeful action.	Teachers are trying various strategies they know or learn about independently. This is inconsistent and creates stress for staff, and unclear boundaries for students.	Implement a clear and consistent student engagement plan. Provide regular feedback to students on their behaviour and acknowledge their efforts. Offer additional support or interventions for students who may need extra guidance.

In the next scenario, we'll apply the Feel + Be = Do formula to enhance staff wellbeing and teamwork (see table 5).

Table 5: Feel + Be = Do: staff wellbeing and teamwork

	Purpose	Current state	Desired state
Feel	To understand how staff are feeling and how they would like to feel.	Staff members feel isolated and stressed due to a lack of collaboration and support.	Staff members feel valued, motivated and part of a supportive team.

	Purpose	Current state	Desired state
Be	To observe the behaviours staff are exhibiting and whether these are helpful, sustainable and reflective of the desired culture.	Staff members work in isolation, resist change and lack communication and cooperation.	Staff members actively engage in collaborative initiatives, share ideas and support each other's professional development.
Do	To use the above to derive meaningful and purposeful action.	Staff spend most of their working time alone. There is limited opportunity for collaboration. No clear expectations or guidelines exist for staff to collaborate.	Develop expectations and guidelines for staff collaboration. Create structures for staff to share ideas, collaborate on projects and provide feedback. Provide ways for staff to actively participate in collaborative tasks.

Feel + Be = Do is a formula for promoting a well culture in the workplace. By focusing on emotions and behaviours before actions, you can create an environment where people feel valued, exhibit positive behaviours and take action that contributes to a healthier and more productive work culture.

The challenge to rest

Just as important as taking intentional action is to figure out how you and your staff can do less, de-implement and slow down. The only way to ensure our profession becomes sustainable is to purposefully slow down, to rest and to make space for ourselves so that we function well when we work.

While the antonyms of the word 'work' are 'leisure' and 'rest', we shouldn't be seeing these as mutually exclusive. In a wellbeing-centred workplace, we use leisure and rest to support the work we do, making it part of how we work well.

I understand this idea is challenging. I used to approach my career in an all-work, no-play kind of way, and I encouraged others to do the same. I would tell myself I needed to earn my rest before I could actually take it. I thought work and rest could not be seen together, that it was one or the other. I thought that working meant doing tasks, teaching or attending meetings, and resting was doing nothing. What I know now is that it is not one or the other. In fact, the more we can find different ways to rest, the more our wellbeing and ability to work well increases.

Resting gives us the chance to break from the daily grind, to remove our mind from the constant thinking about students, planning, resourcing and marking. It allows us to tap into different parts of our brain, invoking a sense of calm, freedom or creativity.

According to Saundra Dalton-Smith, author of *Sacred Rest: Recover Your Life, Renew Your Energy, Restore Your Sanity*, there are seven different types of rest we all need and that many of us are lacking. These include creative rest, emotional rest, mental rest, physical rest, sensory rest, social rest and spiritual rest. Interestingly, sleep is not included in one of the seven types of rest, yet many of us think this, or doing nothing, is what rest is, when in fact this is not accurate at all.

We need to understand that working well and resting go hand-in-hand. If we fail to rest in different ways, our happiness, relationships, creativity and productivity can be negatively impacted. This is true in my experience. As much as I loved teaching, because I failed to rest I wasn't able to work well. When we lack creative rest, we struggle to think of new ideas. When we lack emotional rest, we bottle feelings and emotions up and they weigh us down. When we lack mental rest, we have trouble switching off which can also impact our sleep. When we lack physical rest, we may feel tired or experience muscle aches and pains. When we lack sensory rest, we may become irritable and agitated as the day goes on. When we lack social rest, we may feel like we are always giving and not receiving or that our interactions lack positivity. When we lack spiritual rest, we may struggle to feel as if we have meaning or purpose.

As uncomfortable or impossible as it may seem to implement rest, there is no denying we need it. The challenge is in shifting our mindset from thinking we can only rest on weekends or in school holidays. This way of thinking is not healthy, helpful or sustainable. Instead, we need to make rest a daily occurrence, in micro-moments, to keep our energy up and ensure we work well. Table 6 outlines how this can be done in schools. Note these are just examples of how to support rest. As leaders, ask yourself what can be done to ensure all staff, including you, are able to do these things throughout the day or when needed.

Table 6: Strategies to enable the seven types of rest in schools
Adapted from Dalton-Smith, 2021.

Type of rest	Description	Example strategies
Creative rest	Creative rest reawakens the awe and wonder inside each of us. This could include going out into nature to experience awe and beauty, and filling your workspace with creativity and inspiration.	Design your workspace and classroom so that they inspire. This doesn't necessarily mean plastering the walls with motivating quotes. It's about creating spaces that support and inspire you to think and work well. Take time to go outdoors and move away from the inside environment to find beauty.
Emotional rest	Emotional rest means having the time and space to freely express your feelings, and reduce people-pleasing. Emotional rest requires the courage to be authentic, sharing hard things that otherwise go unsaid.	Ensure you express your feelings and emotions honestly. In teams, provide safe, structured ways for this to occur. Engage in ways to build emotional intelligence of self and others, giving people the tools to share, express and discuss how they and others are feeling. This can also be done with a counsellor, psychologist or trusted colleague.
Mental rest	Mental rest helps us to slow our mind down and switch off.	Ensure you have scheduled breaks. Rather than continually going without a break until students leave for the day, take five to ten minutes every two hours to pause.

Type of rest	Description	Example strategies
Physical rest	Physical rest can be passive or active. Passive physical rest includes sleeping and napping, while active physical rest could mean restorative activities such as yoga, stretching and massage therapy that help improve the body's circulation and flexibility.	Make sure you move and stretch often. When it comes to sleep, I do know some who can find time to have a ten-minute nap at work. If this isn't for you, ensure you work on sleep hygiene and get the right amount of sleep you need each night.
Sensory rest	Our senses are working all the time. Bright lights, computer screens, background noise and multiple conversations can cause our senses to feel overwhelmed.	Closing your eyes for a minute or two in the middle of the day, as well as intentionally unplugging from electronics at the end of the day, helps to counteract this. Shut down screens when you can (ideally a few times a day and one hour before bed), close your eyes for a few moments, pop on noise-cancelling headphones when you need quiet (obviously not while teaching), and reduce bright lights in favour of more natural light.
Social rest	Social rest requires us to surround ourselves with positive and supportive people, reducing interactions with negative and draining people.	Find ways to boost positive, meaningful relationships that make you feel good. Consider the interactions you have within teams, with students and other colleagues, and as a whole staff cohort.
Spiritual rest	Spiritual rest is the ability to feel a deep sense of belonging, love, acceptance and purpose.	Engage in something greater than yourself and add prayer, meditation or community involvement to your daily routine. Look for opportunities to go beyond your physical and mental self. In a faith-based school this may be through prayer, or you may engage in mindfulness and meditation or find ways to contribute to a school event.

Once we learn to identify and support each of these areas, not only are we normalising rest, but we will be in a much better position to create a wellbeing-centred workplace.

Chapter summary

- We need to ensure that everyone – educators, leaders and all school staff – understand what it means to address and improve staff wellbeing. We must challenge previously held ideals about what wellbeing means and be specific about how we're prioritising wellbeing in the workplace.
- We need to rethink and reconsider how we create change, make decisions and plan for new initiatives, moving from student-centred decision-making to a combined approach with staff-wellbeing-centred decision-making.
- To only focus on doing means we are always adding.
- We need to dream up new solutions, identify limitations and ask better questions, leading to change.
- There are seven different types of rest we all need: creative rest, emotional rest, mental rest, physical rest, sensory rest, social rest and spiritual rest.

From theory to action

Staff wellbeing audit

Knowing what impacts staff wellbeing in your school is crucial. Part of this conversation involves identifying limitations, questions to ask and possible solutions. Use the below template to facilitate this with staff.

What areas are impacting staff wellbeing?	
Which area, if addressed, would give us the biggest return on investment? (Choose one.)	

What are the questions we need to ask to understand this better? (You may like to use Feel + Be = Do here.)	
What are our ideas, dreams or possibilities for change?	
What do we have the time, energy and capacity to implement?	

Valuing rest

Rest is essential. What are some ways you can build in micro-opportunities for yourself and staff to rest? You can do this activity with all staff or in teams.

Type of rest	What does this look like?	What support, structures or resources do we need?
Creative rest		
Emotional rest		
Mental rest		
Physical rest		
Sensory rest		
Social rest		
Spiritual rest		

Chapter 4

Perspective
Knowing Yourself as a Leader

Any leader will tell you that there are many skills and strategies you need to learn when you take the leap from classroom teacher to leader. When you go from leading students to leading staff there are so many things to learn, do and understand. As a leader you need to know what is happening in each classroom, the intricacies of the pedagogical approaches across your school, and the names of far more students (and parents) than ever before. Add to this the art of leading others and building relationships with colleagues. It's a huge shift from classroom teacher to leader, and one I am not sure any of us are well prepared for.

When I first took up a leadership role, the only qualification I had was my bachelor's degree in primary education. My degree did not prepare me for leadership. In fact, leadership was not discussed at all. Yet here I was, with my teaching degree and a significant amount of enthusiasm to work well, drive change and make the school I was in the best it could be.

When I stepped into leadership, I didn't realise just how diverse my skill set needed to be. I wasn't prepared for the fact that enthusiasm, dedication and being a great teacher was not enough to successfully lead others. I needed to learn how to develop my head and heart skills – things such as emotional intelligence, connection, compassion and patience. I needed to understand how to lead others, and how people's culture and values influence who they are and how they interact with others. I needed to realise that driving change required far more than having a good idea.

It took me a long time to understand that a great classroom teacher does not equal a great leader. Leadership is something you have to learn and develop over a number of years. When I reflect on my leadership skills now compared to when I first began, there are plenty of things I could have done better back then.

As a new leader, I completely underestimated how interconnected the different roles across a school are. For so long it had been me, in my classroom, with my teaching team. I wasn't aware of all of the other groups of people and the roles they played. I obviously knew they were there and part of our staff, but I had no awareness of how many cogs were spinning to ensure a school functioned well. I also didn't realise that, as a leader, I would need to be aware of the intricacies of every single cog and how they contributed to the school dynamics.

Whether we realise it or not, we rely on each person in a school to feel well, work well, team well and lead well so we can do all of these things well, too. What we often neglect to realise, though, is that we too are a cog in the complex machine that allows a school to function successfully. That means we need to look at who we are being to ensure our part of the machine is working well – that we're supporting others and not being the reason some cogs stop turning. It starts with self-awareness and beliefs.

Self-awareness

Self-awareness is one of those overused, misunderstood terms, much like wellbeing. Like wellbeing, self-awareness requires us to do the work, take responsibility and, at times, get our hands dirty as we engage in self-evaluation. This is how we identify what aligns with who we want to be, and what doesn't.

The creators of self-awareness theory, Shelley Duval and Robert Wicklund (1972), define self-awareness as:

> *The ability to focus on yourself and how your actions, thoughts, or emotions do or don't align with your internal standards. If you're highly self-aware, you can objectively evaluate yourself, manage your emotions, align your behavior with your values, and understand correctly how others perceive you.*

To further expand on self-awareness we also need to know there are two different types of self-awareness. According to a large study conducted by organisational psychologist Tasha Eurich (2018), we have capacity for internal and external self-awareness. Internal self-awareness is how we perceive our values, passions, aspirations, fit with our environment, reactions (including thoughts, feelings, behaviours, strengths and weaknesses), and impact on others. External self-awareness is our ability to understand how others see us in relation to these things.

As leaders it's crucial for us to prioritise building our internal and external self-awareness. This means making time to reflect on ourselves as leaders and to seek feedback from others. The more we understand ourselves as others see us, the more able we are to ensure our leadership approach and style is meeting others' needs, thereby enhancing staff wellbeing.

Eurich (2018) also shares that being high in one type of self-awareness does not make you high in the other. She says we tend to fall into one of four self-awareness archetypes: introspectors, aware, seekers and pleasers. Figure 5 (overleaf) shows how each of these archetypes might play out and how it impacts their ability to lead staff wellbeing.

In all of the schools I have worked at, my wellbeing was at its best where culture too was at its best. However, over time, I realised more and more that who I was being, how I was showing up, and my own beliefs, behaviours, actions, habits, experiences and ways of working with others also impacted my wellbeing, and that of those around me. This is self-awareness. Over time I began to realise how much I was influencing and impacting what was happening around me. I went from thinking things were happening *to* me to realising things were happening *because of* me, and I perhaps had far more control and influence than I would have once liked to have realised. Once I took ownership of this realisation, everything began to shift. I realised that I needed to take responsibility for so many things impacting my wellbeing and ability to lead well. I needed to believe I could make changes, and accept things I couldn't. I had to learn new skills, strategies and ways of thinking while building my self-worth. I had to extend to myself an extensive amount of self-compassion as I began to shift how I showed up at work and home, and how I was leading others. I had to make time and space for self-care and rest, and prioritise what I needed so I could show up better for others.

Figure 5: Self-awareness archetypes
Adapted from Eurich, 2018.

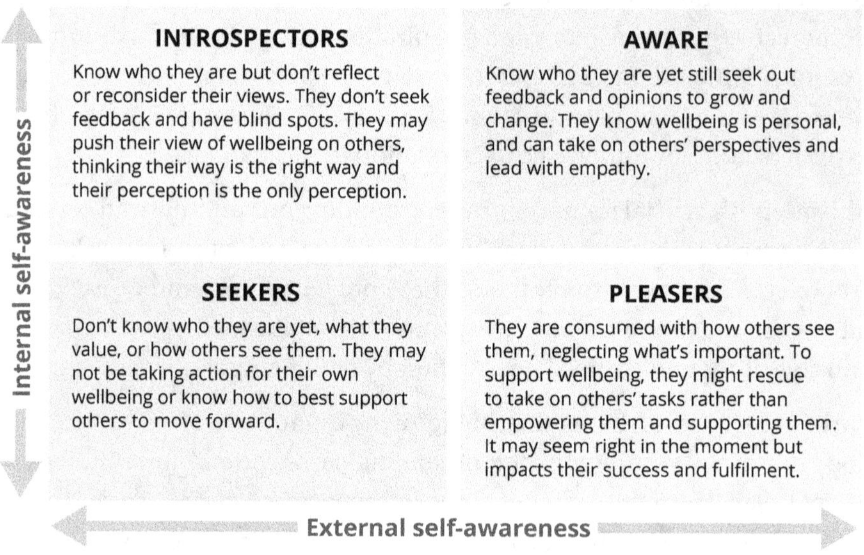

↑ Internal self-awareness ↓

INTROSPECTORS	**AWARE**
Know who they are but don't reflect or reconsider their views. They don't seek feedback and have blind spots. They may push their view of wellbeing on others, thinking their way is the right way and their perception is the only perception.	Know who they are yet still seek out feedback and opinions to grow and change. They know wellbeing is personal, and can take on others' perspectives and lead with empathy.
SEEKERS	**PLEASERS**
Don't know who they are yet, what they value, or how others see them. They may not be taking action for their own wellbeing or know how to best support others to move forward.	They are consumed with how others see them, neglecting what's important. To support wellbeing, they might rescue to take on others' tasks rather than empowering them and supporting them. It may seem right in the moment but impacts their success and fulfilment.

← **External self-awareness** →

This realisation was only possible because I developed my self-awareness, but it didn't happen instantly. It required openness, practice, patience, a whole lot of unlearning and relearning, and help from some wonderful coaches and mentors. As well as this, I had to embrace what I refer to as the seven selves of self-awareness (see figure 6).

While you may be familiar with these seven areas on their own, you might not know they play a key role in developing your ability to embrace wellbeing leadership. Wellbeing leadership is not just about leading others, but also about how you lead yourself. To do this well, you need to always be advancing your self-awareness, and looking at the different areas that help you to do so. Let's take a look at the seven selves of self-awareness, what they mean and how they apply to wellbeing leadership.

Figure 6: The seven selves of self-awareness

Self-care

Self-care is looking after our physical, mental and emotional selves. This includes activities and daily habits such as sleep, exercise, nutrition and meditation, and can also extend to more hedonistic activities such as massages and holidays. Ultimately, it is time and space allocated to prioritising our mental, physical and emotional needs, which I recommend doing regularly.

While we are quick to consider others' self-care needs, we also need to do this for ourselves. We can not lead as our best selves if we are low on energy, not eating well or lacking sleep. Without true and planned self-care practices, we can find ourselves pushed to the limit with very little in our tank. Prioritising daily self-care is a must for any leader.

Self-compassion

Self-compassion means extending the same kindness to yourself as you would others. Research psychologist Dr Kristin Neff (2024) shares that 'self-compassion involves acting the same way towards yourself when you are having a difficult time, fail, or notice something you don't like about yourself' as you would a friend. She says we should let go of 'stiff-upper-lip' mentality, and instead say to ourselves things such as 'This is really difficult right now. How can I comfort and care for myself at this moment?'

Without self-compassion we can be extremely hard on ourselves as leaders. However, we have to acknowledge that many of us in education have not received the leadership training required to do our job well. This isn't our fault; it's a flaw in the system. Kirstin Ferguson (2023), Australian leadership researcher and author of *Head and Heart*, shares that on average a person may be in a leadership role for 13 years before being offered any formal leadership training. She found that training is often reserved for those already in senior positions, meaning those moving into leadership miss the crucial guidance they require. With this in mind, we have to utilise significant amounts of self-compassion as we navigate a job we are likely underprepared, under-skilled and under-resourced for.

Self-worth

Self-worth is the internal sense of being good enough and worthy of love and belonging (UNWC, n.d.). Self-worth is often confused with self-esteem, but they are two different things. Self-esteem relies on external factors such as successes and achievements to define worth and can often be inconsistent, leading to someone struggling with feeling worthy. We need to recognise that self-worth comes from within and can only be established through internal resources. It does not come from outside of us, from others or from recognition or appreciation.

As leaders we need to build our self-worth and support others in doing so. Just like self-compassion, we are most likely great at encouraging others to recognise their self-worth, but perhaps not so great in building our own. Increasing self-worth, and knowing we truly matter, belong and are worthy, can be challenging.

I suggest trying the following strategies (adapted from Gupta, 2023):

- **Do things you enjoy and are good at:** This reinforces your proficiency and capability.

- **Exercise and challenge yourself:** Physical activity is linked to a greater sense of self-worth, as is the act of striving towards goals.
- **Challenge negative thoughts:** Next time you catch yourself thinking negatively about yourself, think of an alternative realistic thought to replace it.
- **Seek support:** From a therapist or mentor.

Self-development

Self-development has become one of the fastest-growing industries, with personal development books among the top selling in the world (Bidilică, 2024). Self-development is a key part of self-awareness. As we embark on developing ourselves, we increase our ability to be more self-aware, as we unlearn, relearn, learn new things and grow. Self-development is closely linked with professional development, and at times these can overlap – especially within the space of leadership skills. Self-development can include focusing on a vast range of skills, all of which support us to increase our chances of success, achieve our goals and manifest our dreams (Davis, 2023).

The Berkeley Well-being Institute has identified nine skills that are essential to any self-development plan (Davis, 2023). These skills are not only essential to life, but also to how we lead. While there are many other areas that could be listed here, these nine link to wellbeing leadership while also relating to physical, mental and emotional health (see table 7).

Table 7: Nine self-development skills
Adapted from Davis, 2023.

Physical health	Mental health	Emotional health
Develop a healthier relationship with your phone. Take care of your health.	Establish a growth mindset. Develop your ability to think like an entrepreneur. Develop yourself to be more resilient. Keep developing yourself in new ways.	Calm yourself and de-stress. Develop your positivity reflex. Stay mindful of the present moment.

Self-efficacy

As educators, we are very familiar with the term 'collective efficacy' in relation to student learning, yet we don't often realise developing self-efficacy is a key element of wellbeing leadership. Self-efficacy is the belief you hold that you can complete a certain task successfully and achieve the intended outcome. Ultimately, high self-efficacy means believing ourselves to be capable of carrying out tasks without any fear, doubt or worry. Our level of self-efficacy also reflects our confidence in our ability to exert control over our own motivation, behaviour and social environment (Carey and Forsyth, 2009).

The most important piece for self-efficacy in relation to wellbeing leadership is the connection between this and motivation, behaviour and social environment. The more we are able to build self-efficacy, the better we understand why we are doing something, how we are behaving and who this impacts. It influences the why, how and who of our day-to-day leadership.

Self-acceptance

According to Elizabeth Perry (2021):

> *Self-acceptance is the act of accepting yourself and all your personality traits exactly as they are. You accept them no matter whether they are positive or negative. This includes your physical and mental attributes. It means recognising that your value goes beyond your personal attributes and actions.*

The more we can step into self-acceptance, the more we can truly acknowledge who we are and how we are relating to others. While it may not be easy to begin with, self-acceptance comes with an immense sense of freedom to be more, to evolve and let go of the stories that hold us back.

As we carry out different leadership responsibilities, we become aware of aspects of ourselves that we view as negative and wish we didn't possess. As wellbeing leaders we need to model acceptance of all parts of who we are. This means at times being open about our positive and negative aspects and what these look like. Through modelling self-acceptance we can help others to let go of obstacles and show them what follows when we hold no self-judgement.

Self-responsibility

Self-responsibility is the accountability we have for our past or future actions (responsibility can be retrospective and prospective). Self-responsibility is also very closely linked to autonomy in that it requires us to be self-conscious, self-reflective and self-determining, as we exercise our ability to deliberate, judge, choose and act in certain ways (Maier 2019).

As leaders, self-responsibility is something to practise and model. Taking the past and future into account, we need to be willing to take responsibility for any decisions we make and actions we take. This includes everything from significant decisions to everyday decisions we make that support our personal wellbeing. The more we are able to take responsibility for our actions and decisions without judgement, excuse-making or denial, the more we demonstrate how to lead with wellbeing in mind. Modelling this to those we lead provides a clear demonstration of wellbeing leadership.

Ongoing practice

The seven selves are not designed to be prescriptive steps or things to do all at once. As wellbeing leaders they should become part of our ongoing practice, allowing us to develop our self-awareness and lead more openly over time. They should become part of our ongoing reflection as leaders and continue to be apparent in our day-to-day routines and habits. Consistently engaging in and reflecting on the seven selves allows us to build self-awareness over time and make subtle changes frequently, leading to big changes over the longer term.

I found that once I had established a higher sense of self-awareness through utilising the seven selves, changing my daily habits, behaviours, approaches and practices, and continually reflecting on them, things started to shift. I became more aware of how I connected with others and the intention I had for each interaction, rather than being completely task oriented. I invested in self-development for personal and professional gains. Self-care practices became part of my daily habits via things such as nourishing foods and time to rest. I accepted the things I could and couldn't control and became far less judgemental and far more self-compassionate.

I often reflect on the period of growth I experienced while doing this work and have so much gratitude for it. It really was the time in which my life, personally and professionally, started to transform. When I think of all the moments, experiences and challenges that helped to make this transformation occur, I can see it wasn't easy. In fact, it was a long, windy road and I had a lot to learn. These learnings, though, shaped who I am now – the person I am and the leader I am. They also helped me to learn what I needed, what mattered for my own wellbeing, and what mattered for me to be able to lead with wellbeing in mind.

Here are some of my biggest learnings through developing self-awareness:

- I could identify what I needed for my wellbeing.
- I recognised what I was responsible for and took accountability for it.
- I recognised what I couldn't control or influence, and let these things go, shifting my energy to things I had influence and control over.
- I stopped blaming, making excuses and looking for reasons why things couldn't be a certain way or why I couldn't do things.
- I built more sustainable habits that supported who I wanted to be.
- I worked on my own beliefs and mindset.
- I realised that even if things in a school setting weren't great, there was so much I could do to ensure my experiences were ones that I wanted to have.
- I stopped outsourcing my wellbeing to others or external circumstances, and I took 100 per cent responsibility for everything I could.

In some ways you could say I shifted from a fixed to a growth mindset. Looking back, it was hard, vulnerable work. It was not a quick-fix fun activity. It took a significant level of commitment, openness and willingness to recognise the pieces of me I liked and wanted to keep, and the pieces of me that I was no longer proud of – things that didn't serve me anymore and that were unhelpful to my wellbeing and leadership.

You can do this, too.

Beliefs

Along with my advancement in self-awareness, I also looked at my beliefs – particularly those I had about being an educator, a leader and working in schools. The curiosity I approached this work with was only possibly due to my expanding self-awareness, and it had a profound impact on my ability to lead well.

A belief is a deeply ingrained perspective or conviction that a person holds about certain aspects of life, people, situations or the world at large. Beliefs are often formed through a combination of personal experiences, upbringing, cultural influences and exposure to information. Beliefs play a pivotal role in shaping how we interpret events, make decisions and interact with our environment. They provide us with a lens through which we view the world. As much as our beliefs are part of who we are, they are not based on fact or truth.

Whether we're conscious of it or not, our beliefs play a major role in our personal, team and workplace cultures. Our beliefs hold a certain power over us, influencing how we decipher, make meaning of, and respond to the world around us. They underpin how we think things ought to be, our priorities, and where we invest our resources. They guide us towards a particular way of living, whether we know it or not.

Beliefs fall into two categories: helpful beliefs or hindering beliefs. A helpful belief is a positive and constructive belief. It supports us to grow, improves resilience and contributes to our overall wellbeing. Supportive beliefs encourage proactive behaviours, contribute to a positive outlook and empower us to overcome challenges.

Examples of helpful beliefs include:

- All students can learn.
- Exercise is good for me, even though it can be hard.
- Work/life flow is possible and a must.
- Rest is essential for productivity.
- Openness and vulnerability are strengths each person should embrace.
- Change brings new opportunities and growth.
- I can implement work boundaries and still do my job well.

- I can empower those I lead by building their capacity even if it is challenging in the beginning.
- Being open about my wellbeing helps others understand me.
- If I ask more questions I can better support those I lead.
- Asking for help makes me a better leader.

Hindering beliefs are the opposite of helpful beliefs. A hindering belief can undermine our confidence, hold us back or prevent us from pursuing opportunities. Hindering beliefs have the power to shape thoughts, emotions and behaviours, leading to self-doubt, avoidance of challenges and fear of failure. Over time, they can deter us from taking risks, trying new things and embracing change.

We all have beliefs that are hindering, yet many of us are unaware of them. They are hidden in the conversations we have, they drive the assumptions we make, and they influence our actions without us even knowing. Building awareness of our beliefs is an incredible opportunity to reflect and be curious about how and why we do the things we do. We can perhaps even work to change these beliefs and the behaviours that go with them.

Examples of hindering beliefs include:

- A student's ability to learn is determined by their parents' career choice.
- Work and personal life should be separate.
- The longer you work the better you will be.
- I need to put others' needs before mine.
- Exercise is hard.
- Work has to come first if I want to be seen as committed.
- The only way to get a leadership role is to work harder.
- As a leader I need to do things that might be stressful for others.
- Great leaders make decisions alone.
- As a leader I need to arrive at work first and leave after other staff leave.
- My wellbeing comes after that of my staff.

Being aware of both helpful and hindering beliefs can help us move forward and face challenges head-on, rather than becoming stuck in our ways with no confidence or willingness to do things differently.

In my early days of teaching and even as a leader, I held some beliefs that now go against what I believe and the work I do. I want to share these with you so you can see that, while we may all want to be our best selves for our staff and work with the best intentions, it may not always come across that way. I also want to share these with you to let you know that beliefs are not fact, and you have the power to lean in, be curious and change what you believe.

Beliefs I have had include:

- The more hours I put in the easier it becomes.
- Arriving early and leaving late means I am a dedicated employee.
- Working weekends is normal for teachers.
- Burnout is inevitable.
- Taking time off (a sick day) isn't the right thing to do.
- I can rest during the holidays, not term time.
- Student success is all that matters.
- I need to earn my self-care. My students need me more than I need me.
- There will always be something else to do, so keep going.

I am not sure where these beliefs came from, but they were certainly loud and clear. Perhaps I learned them from my early mentors or leaders, or from my family. Perhaps I observed that this was the mentality you needed in order to be successful. Maybe it came from movies where leaders and CEOs were portrayed as having no life outside of work, work needing to be the number one priority, and there being no room for compassion, empathy or going slowly. Wherever the beliefs came from, they shaped my life and career.

I believed this way of thinking and working was the only way to succeed and be happy, but it actually did me far more harm than good. It impacted my ability to connect with others and to value and act with compassion. It saw me focus on tasks and things we needed to do, with this being my main reason for connecting with colleagues – too often asking, 'Have you got the resource for this morning?' rather than, 'How was your weekend?' It saw me be rigid in my thinking, not having the ability to be flexible or take on new ideas. I also struggled to support those I led because I didn't take the time to get to know them. As far as I was concerned, we had a job to do and everything else could wait.

(Note: I would like to take a minute to apologise to those I worked with and led throughout my career. Especially if I ever made you feel like you didn't matter, like you weren't enough, or that I didn't have time for you. It was not about you. I was making it about me, and for that I am sorry.)

I can recall numerous times in which my beliefs were core to an issue with a colleague or team I was a part of (not that I knew it at the time). One that will always be clear in my mind was when a leader shared that one of my colleagues felt I didn't like them because I never asked how their weekend was or about their children. This confession from my then colleague led to a meeting with our leader to help us talk through how we were both feeling. As hard as it was to hear that I had made someone feel like they weren't good enough or that I didn't have time for them, this was one of the most valuable conversations I ever had in my career. It was a challenging conversation for all, including the leader facilitating it, and I am forever grateful that it was brought to my attention. Upon reflection, this conversation was part of what sparked my journey to become more self-aware. It made me reflect on many interactions I had with colleagues, in the past and present. I realised that there were definitely moments where, even though unintentionally, I may have come across like I didn't care. This was a hard truth to learn. It was also a moment in which I could choose to ignore what I was seeing and move on, staying the way I was, blaming others or making it their problem or see this as an opportunity to do things differently.

Following this experience, I made it a priority to get to know my colleagues as people first, and teachers second. I think sometimes we forget this: that we aren't just teachers, we are people with families, lives, interests, hobbies and challenges that impact who we are, how we feel and how we work. I began to ask my colleagues about their weekend. I started to pay more attention to what they shared, making a mental note to follow up with them about their holiday, grand final game or their child's first dance event. I wanted them to know I saw them as a person, and didn't just think they were a teacher and nothing else, disregarding who they were outside the school environment.

As educators we often talk about how important it is to build relationships with our students, to have connection before content, but we don't apply the same to our colleagues. I think this needs to change. We need to give dedicated time to getting to know one another, to build relationships and positive connections. We need a chance to get to know one another's strengths and how each of us likes to work, our boundaries and beliefs. When we do this, we will undoubtedly have more open and safe relationships and see trust, collaboration and cohesion increase – all of which will positively impact wellbeing.

Additionally, the individual beliefs we have will influence our collective beliefs. It is important to know what our beliefs are, and encourage our staff to do the same, to ensure our individual beliefs support the workplace we are trying to create. If we don't address this, and a significant number of staff members have beliefs that are holding them back, this could be silently paralysing performance and affecting our entire school (Wright, 2023).

Chapter summary

- Self-awareness is essential to wellbeing leadership.
- Self-awareness for wellbeing leadership includes the seven selves: self-care, self-compassion, self-worth, self-development, self-efficacy, self-acceptance and self-responsibility.
- Building self-awareness is a skill and practice that needs to be ongoing and part of wellbeing leadership.
- Beliefs are not truths, yet they shape our behaviours and actions.
- We have many beliefs but may not be aware that they exist or know how they impact us or others.
- Beliefs can be helpful or hindering, and when needed we can shift these to support us.

From theory to action

Increasing self-awareness

Revisit the seven selves of self-awareness and ask yourself the following questions:

- Which ones do I do well?
- Which ones do I need to improve?

- Of all of these, which is most important for me to focus on right now?
- If I do this, how will it benefit me?
- If I don't do this, what will happen?

Building better beliefs

Choose a topic you want to explore, such as being a great leader. Ask yourself what your beliefs are around that topic; for example, 'What do I believe about being a great leader?' (You can choose any topic here – for example, exercise, money, success and so on.) Allow yourself around five minutes to list all your beliefs about your chosen topic.

Then, look at each belief and consider the following questions:

- What evidence do I have to know this is true?
- How does this belief impact my work?
- What could happen if this isn't true?
- Is there a more helpful belief I could foster?

Using your responses to these questions, sort your beliefs into lists of helpful or hindering.

For example:

Hindering beliefs	Helpful beliefs
The more hours I put in the easier it becomes.	I should be able to rest when needed.
Arriving early and leaving late means I am a dedicated leader.	I use the time I have available intentionally.
Working weekends is normal for leaders.	
Taking time off (a sick day) isn't the right thing to do.	
I can rest during the holidays, not term time.	
Student needs are all that matter.	
I need to earn self-care.	
There will always be something else to do, so keep going.	

Then, review your hindering beliefs and shift them to helpful.

For example:

Hindering beliefs	Helpful beliefs
The more hours I put in the easier it becomes.	I put in the hours I am required to and am efficient with the time I have.
Arriving early and leaving late means I am a dedicated leader.	I am dedicated and work as needed.
Working weekends is normal for leaders.	Weekends are for me. Modelling work boundaries is useful for my staff to see.
Taking time off (a sick day) isn't the right thing to do.	If I am sick I take a day off.
I can rest during the holidays, not term time.	Daily rest is essential.
Student needs are all that matter.	Staff needs matter as well as student needs.
I need to earn self-care.	Self-care is available whenever I need it.
There will always be something else to do, so keep going.	I manage tasks by focusing on what is important and urgent first.

Then, reflect on your new beliefs and note how they will impact and influence your life:

For example:

New helpful belief	Impact and influence
I put in the hours I am required to and am efficient with the time I have.	I am mindful of how much I am working. It requires me to focus on the time I have and the tasks I need to do, not worry about working all the time.
I am dedicated and work as needed.	Each thing I do is because I am dedicated.
Weekends are for me. Modelling work boundaries is useful for my staff to see.	Weekends are space for me and I utilise them as such.

New helpful belief	Impact and influence
If I am sick I take a day off.	When I'm sick, I rest, which helps me recover.
Daily rest is essential.	Each day I make and find time for rest even if it is five to ten minutes.
Staff needs matter as well as student needs.	I create ways for all staff to feel happy, safe and productive.
Self-care is available whenever I need it.	I create daily and weekly self-care habits to support my wellbeing.
I manage tasks by focusing on what is important and urgent first.	I look at my list and prioritise things on it, working on what is essential only, being okay with having other things wait.

This exercise is an example related to individual beliefs, but you can adapt it to use in teams and with all staff.

Chapter 5

People
Wellbeing is Culture

A wellbeing-centred workplace is one that has a positive culture. How your staff feel, work, team and lead *is culture*. Staff wellbeing is the missing link in many schools' attempts to improve culture.

Up until now schools have seen culture as separate from staff wellbeing. But if culture reflects our workplace, and wellbeing supports our people, perhaps this is not so much about either/or but *both* – the culture of our workplace and the wellbeing of our people combined (see figure 7 overleaf).

Wellbeing and culture go hand-in-hand. It is not one or the other, but both. In its most simple form, we can understand culture to be the what, how and why of a workplace. It encompasses beliefs, values, experiences, actions and behaviours. A positive culture occurs within a safe, connected, productive workplace where staff are valued and fulfilled, and where staff wellbeing thrives. It's evident in how people show up to work, how they relate to one another, and how they offer support and manage conflict. It's about how staff contribute to their teams, conduct themselves in meetings and face challenges.

Figure 7: Wellbeing is culture

According to Cameron et al. (2011) there are six elements that contribute to a positive workplace culture:

1. **Caring:** Colleagues care for one another and treat each other as friends.
2. **Compassionate support:** When others are struggling, people act with kindness and compassion.
3. **Forgiveness:** When mistakes are made, people forgive rather than blame.
4. **Inspiration:** People inspire one another.
5. **Meaning:** Staff are elevated and renewed through meaningful work.
6. **Respect, integrity and gratitude:** People express appreciation, act with integrity and treat each other with respect.

These six areas, while about culture, also connect closely to psychological wellbeing, reminding us that the need to move away from fruit bowls and morning teas (subjective wellbeing) is necessary to create a positive school culture (see figure 8).

I am often asked how we can create a workplace where psychological wellbeing is high, and where we move away from subjective wellbeing strategies as the core solution for staff wellbeing. Even though there is urgency to do this, the answer is not as easy as offering a yoga class or putting a coffee van on at the end of term. It lies in how we build our culture.

Ryan and Deci (2001) describe subjective (hedonic) wellbeing in terms of pleasure attainment and pain avoidance. They say a subjective wellbeing approach focuses on happiness (such as a morning tea or meeting-free week) whereas a psychological (eudaimonic) approach focuses on concepts such as meaning and self-realisation, and whether a person is fully functioning. I think it helps also to consider subjective wellbeing as what is most commonly external to us – a quick fix that brings positive feelings, is pleasure-driven and easy; whereas psychological wellbeing focuses on complex, internally based ideas such as meaning, fulfillment, connection and growth.

Figure 8: Subjective and psychological wellbeing

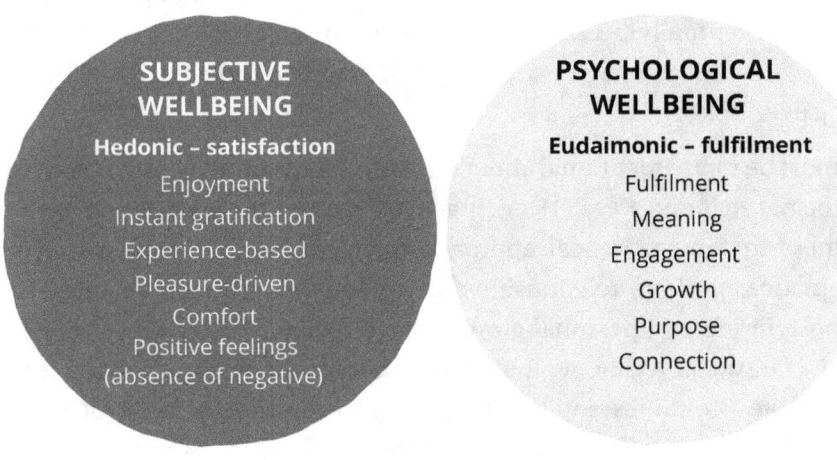

We can see from figure 8 that some of the concepts within subjective wellbeing go against what we know is needed to create a healthy workplace culture. For example, if we continually focus on keeping people comfortable and trying to avoid negative feelings, we will not build a workplace where open, vulnerable conversations exist. If we only focus on enjoyment and instant gratification, we imply wellbeing requires us to do easy and enjoyable work all the time, which isn't an accurate reflection of what it means to work. There are tasks and times where we are required to do things that we don't enjoy and that don't give us that instant feeling of gratification, though this doesn't mean they negatively impact our wellbeing.

It is becoming more accepted that the approach of using isolated subjective wellbeing strategies is not enough, yet building approaches to enhance psychological wellbeing is something many schools are yet to address. Ad-hoc activities, wellbeing weeks and stress-management workshops are conducted frequently, yet allowing ourselves and our staff time to explore who we are, how we are behaving, the experiences we want to cultivate, our beliefs and values, and building self-awareness is overlooked. We are ignoring the fact that wellbeing is culture, and it's what needs to be prioritised to create a healthy and well workplace. You can conduct as many wellbeing activities as you like, but unless you build the foundation of a positive workplace culture alongside these, they will eventually become undervalued and lose the desired impact due to the novelty factor wearing off, and psychological wellbeing being overlooked.

We must be more intentional about building and promoting psychological wellbeing. Ryff and Keys (1995) suggest there are six key dimensions of wellness in the theoretical approach to psychological wellbeing: self-acceptance, positive relationships, autonomy, environmental mastery, purpose in life and personal growth. If we focus on these areas we can build a culture of wellbeing that allows staff to feel, work, team and lead well. Table 8 outlines some activities and exercises for each of these dimensions you can try in your workplace.

As you can see, by utilising Ryff and Keys' six key dimensions we can begin to create a harmonious workplace where beliefs, values, awareness and experiences coexist to support the multiple dimensions needed to create an environment where staff wellbeing is valued and intertwined into the daily aspects that influence overall culture. Cameron et al.'s six elements that contribute to a positive workplace culture – caring, compassionate support, forgiveness, inspiration, meaning, and respect, integrity and gratitude – naturally align with Ryff and Keys' work.

Although it may seem like a lot more work than addressing staff wellbeing through a subjective approach such as popping some chocolates on the staffroom table (because, let's be honest, it is), it needs to be done.

Table 8: Psychological dimensions: activities to try
Adapted from Ryff and Keys, 1995.

Application to wellbeing leadership	Activities to try
1. Self-acceptance	
Promote self-forgiveness and self-compassion. Find ways to share both positive and challenging things by reflecting and reviewing goals. Reflect on and appreciate experiences from the past, fostering resilience and a sense of optimism.	Self-positivity activity: Have everyone write down three things they appreciate about themselves and share them with a partner or in a team meeting. Acceptance exercise: Conduct a 'strengths and growth areas' discussion where team members openly acknowledge both their positive attributes and areas for improvement without judgement. Positive reflection task: Allocate time for people to individually reflect on a recent success or achievement and share it with the team during a weekly check-in meeting.
2. Positive relationships	
Focus on creating relationships built on integrity and shared values. Make time for team members to get to know one another, encouraging open communication. Encourage acts of kindness and provide support for colleagues in need. Promote collaboration, appreciative listening and reciprocity across the workplace.	Values workshop: Host sessions where everyone defines shared values, fostering integrity in relationships. Team-bonding events: Arrange activities for teams to mingle and communicate openly, building trust and understanding. Kindness initiative: Start a campaign for acts of kindness among colleagues, promoting support and empathy. Collaboration workshops: Conduct sessions to enhance collaboration and listening skills, encouraging reciprocity in the workplace.

Application to wellbeing leadership	Activities to try
3. Autonomy	
Provide tools and resources for individuals to take ownership of their work and decisions. Help staff develop skills to resist pressure and maintain their individuality in the workplace. Build capacity to regulate emotions and develop emotional awareness and agility. Assist staff to evaluate behaviours and alignment with values.	Empowerment workshops: Organise workshops to promote autonomy and see where independent decision-making could be applied. Resilience training: Offer training sessions focused on building social resilience and responding to external influences. Emotional regulation exercises: Implement activities or challenges that encourage people to build emotional awareness and agility. This could include how to manage time pressure or stress-management techniques. Values-based reflection sessions: Hold regular reflection sessions where everyone evaluates their actions and decisions based on personal values. Encourage individuals to align their behaviours with their core values, fostering a sense of integrity and purpose in their work.
4. Environmental mastery	
Enhance skills and abilities specific to their role. Implement initiatives that empower staff to have more control over their work activities and decisions. Provide options for flexible scheduling, remote work or job crafting.	Skills workshops: Host regular training sessions targeting specific skill areas to enhance staff competence and mastery in their roles. Empowerment teams: Form cross-functional teams with autonomy to tackle strategic projects, allowing staff to seize opportunities and shape their work activities according to their skills and interests. Flexi-work trial: Implement a temporary program allowing people to choose flexible work arrangements, aligning with their needs and values, to boost job satisfaction and motivation.

Application to wellbeing leadership	Activities to try
5. Purpose in life	
Help everyone define clear and achievable goals, both personally and professionally. Encourage sharing of meaningful experiences or achievements. Encourage people to participate in projects or initiatives that align with their values and beliefs.	Goal-setting workshop: Facilitate a workshop where teams set clear, achievable goals, fostering direction and purpose in their work. Meaningful moments board: Create a board for people to share significant life experiences, promoting reflection and a sense of purpose within the workplace. Purpose-driven projects: Allocate time for everyone to work on projects aligned with organisational values, allowing them to contribute meaningfully and reaffirm their life objectives.
6. Personal growth	
Implement training programs, workshops and skill-development sessions to provide opportunities for staff to expand their knowledge and expertise. Create a culture that values curiosity and innovation, encouraging staff to explore new ideas, projects and experiences both within and outside of their roles. Establish clear pathways for career progression and advancement within the organisation. Introduce practices such as regular self-assessment, feedback sessions and coaching opportunities.	Growth workshops: Host workshops covering various topics such as leadership skills, industry trends and PD. Invite guest speakers and experts to provide insights and facilitate discussions. Innovation challenges: Organise innovation challenges where teams are tasked with proposing and implementing new ideas or initiatives to address current challenges or improve processes. Mentorship program: Establish a formal mentorship program where senior staff mentor junior staff members, providing guidance, support and opportunities for skill development. Self-reflection sessions: Schedule regular self-reflection sessions where people have dedicated time to reflect on their experiences, accomplishments and areas for improvement.

The impact of different cultures

With the make-up of staff being unique to each school, we can't expect that culture will be uniform. Just as wellbeing varies from person to person, team to team and workplace to workplace, so too does culture. It is different from one school to the next based on the people who work there, what they bring, and what they add to their team and the collective culture that exists when all staff come together.

I have worked in schools with positive cultures, and schools where the culture wasn't so great. I have seen culture shift over time, for better and worse. I have worked in schools where staff grew together, where values were established and utilised, and aspects of culture evolved with intentional action. I have worked in schools with wonderful staff, but where changes caused disgruntlement to creep in, trust and integrity to drop and culture to fall apart. I have worked in secondary schools and primary schools, each with their unique nuances influencing school culture. I have worked in low socioeconomic schools, and high-fee-paying independent schools – each with their own successes and challenges. I have worked in numerous states in Australia and in the UK, too. Despite this vast experience, one thing remains true for all workplaces: the school you work at and its culture impact your overall wellbeing – how you feel, teach, work, lead and connect with your colleagues and your students.

When I taught in the UK, I was privileged to be at a school that had mastered the art of high expectations, accountability, rigour in teaching, and performance and feedback cycles, while also maintaining a great culture. Some say that these things can't coexist – that accountability doesn't belong or isn't part of great culture. I can attest that this isn't true; in fact, it's the opposite. In this school, staff would gather in the staffroom to eat lunch, attend social events and be there to support one another personally and professionally, no matter the position they held in the school. This was perhaps one of my happiest and most fulfilling times teaching. In this environment as an educator, I knew what I needed to be doing to do a great job, and everyone in the school had the same shared belief and understanding. I had great relationships with those I worked with – we could go from feedback and performance conversations to after-school dinners without any tension or discomfort. This reflected our shared values and the experiences we cultivated, and I felt like I had ample balance between work and home (I was in the UK, after all, so there was a fair amount of travelling and exploring to be done).

However, I have also experienced the opposite of this. I have worked in schools where 'accountability' and 'feedback' were taboo words, where open connection was absent in favour of exclusive groups that took me back to my high school days. I have been left out of social events and excluded from school activities. I have worked in teams where resources were only shared with some members and not others. I have been asked to attend mediation sessions because I questioned the status quo rather than blindly 'having someone's back'. I have been in meetings where colleagues have yelled, made snide comments and been openly rude, and where people have stormed out of meetings with no follow-up, apology or responsibility taken for their behaviour. I have been in schools where it was more acceptable to keep everyone happy than work to establish a culture where we could positively rumble with one another, be open in dialogue, healthily debate topics and have clear expectations of how we worked together. I didn't have the same level of enjoyment or engagement when I was working in schools where culture was poor. Some days, going to work was really hard, and sometimes I didn't want to go at all.

As you can see, I have seen and experienced a significant amount of positives, negatives and contrasts in my career. And what I can share is this: in a school where culture is well, where staff are positively connected to one another, have shared and aligned beliefs and values, and hold each other accountable to what is important to them as a collective, something magical happens. Engagement increases, support is everywhere, open dialogue is expected, belonging happens naturally and productivity increases. Higher levels of wellbeing are a natural by-product of all these things.

In a school where culture is low, the opposite occurs. Staff are divided, belonging is limited to groups of people rather than all staff, teams compete with one another instead of collaborating, tension is high, resilience is low, and gossip and corridor conversations are rife. Accountability is unclear and confused with micromanaging, and no one is sure when they have done enough. Low levels of wellbeing are very common in places such as this. This reflects that wellbeing and culture go hand-in-hand.

As figure 9 demonstrates, when culture and wellbeing is low, our people operate and function in ways that are not conducive to the environment we are trying to create and the work we are trying to do. When culture and wellbeing is high, the opposite is true. It's also apparent that while 'culture' is a term used to describe the feel of the whole organisation, it is very much dependent on the individuals and teams within it.

Figure 9: Culture and wellbeing

CULTURE ↑		
	There are clear and shared beliefs and values, with all staff committed and working towards the same vision, however, there is a lack of workplace wellbeing strategies utilised due to the strong commitment to work.	There are clear and shared beliefs and values, with all staff committed and working towards the same vision, with staff utilising and feeling balanced in both personal and workplace wellbeing strategies, interventions and approaches applied.
	Vision, values, beliefs and experiences are inconsistent, causing tension and conflict across the workplace, with a lack of workplace wellbeing strategies, interventions and approaches being used individually or collectively.	Vision, values, beliefs and experiences are inconsistent, causing tension and conflict across the workplace, yet people experience a personal sense of fulfilment and meaning, and prioritise their personal wellbeing.

← WELLBEING →

Cultures within cultures

Culture reflects the individuals and teams within a workplace. This means there are several coexisting cultures in every school. For ease and simplicity, it makes sense to focus on workplace culture as a whole; yet it's important to remember that individuals come together to form teams, teams make up larger teams, and all these together form the workplace. This means each person brings their own unique culture, and this culture is present within each team culture. When combined, these individual cultures contribute to the larger workplace culture. However, in the process of building culture, we often overlook individual contributions. We forget to consider how these different cultures fit together or whether they conflict with one another, both within teams and in the wider workplace.

As shown in figure 10, coexisting cultures in the workplace include:

- **Personal culture:** The individual, who they are, their own culture.
- **Team culture:** The culture of a team, such as Year 6 or the Science faculty, made up of multiple personal cultures.
- **Workplace culture:** The culture of all staff, made up of personal cultures and team cultures, i.e. a school.

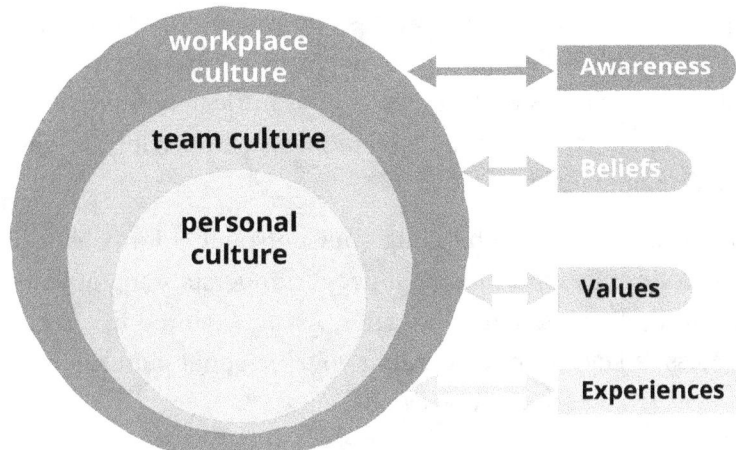

Figure 10: Coexisting cultures in a school

The culture of each team and individual in the school contributes to the overall workplace culture. We can work on our whole school culture through shared and collective beliefs and values, but how well, if at all, do we consider the team and personal cultures that lie within the wider workplace culture?

Personal culture

How aware are you of your personal culture? Do you know how it contributes to who you are and the work that you do?

Personal culture refers to the unique combination of values, beliefs, attitudes, behaviours, experiences and identities that shape who you are and guide your interactions with the world. It is influenced by your upbringing, family background, personal experiences, societal influences, and the way you perceive and respond to various aspects of life. Personal culture plays a significant role in your world view, decision-making processes, communication style and overall sense of self. It is a dynamic and evolving aspect of you that reflects your individuality and how you relate to the broader cultural and social contexts in which you live and work.

According to Melissa Daimler, organisational development and leadership expert and author of *ReCulturing*, a healthy personal culture is one in which behaviours, practices and processes are aligned with values. To achieve this, individuals must define their own values and create a system that prioritises and integrates what's important to them (Daimler, 2021). What this highlights is that each one of us carries our own distinct set of behaviours, values and processes that intricately influence our daily choices, meaning-making and relationships, inevitably extending into our professional realm.

Recognising and comprehending your personal culture, as well as that of your colleagues, can provide a deeper understanding of your actions, motivations, successes and struggles. As we explored in chapter 4, self-awareness is key to understanding your personal culture and how this influences team and workplace culture.

Team culture

What is your team culture made up of? How does this impact workplace culture?

By the most basic definition, team culture is made up of the values, beliefs, behaviours and attitudes shared by a team. It is how people work in tandem towards a common goal and how they treat each other. Just like culture within a society, team culture is influenced by its individual members (Iñiguez, 2023).

At the beginning of each year, many teams go through the process of understanding their team culture and setting intentions about what they want it to be. As a team, you might contemplate your values, norms and preferred working dynamics. Essentially, this process is about shaping a team culture. Yet, for many teams, listing words is as far as this goes – and this is where many teams (and workplaces) fall down. Listing values is easy; putting them into practice is more difficult, and a key step that is often missed (we will cover more on values later in the chapter).

Further to this is considering where team values come from. Are they derived from the team and individuals within the team alone, or do they connect back to the wider workplace values?

Team cultures too can be vastly different across a workplace. Some teams work well together, have a sense of unity with shared values, and all support one another, collaborating and working cohesively without the need for guidance or intervention. Other teams, in the same workplace, can be the complete opposite. They can be dysfunctional, misaligned in values, have conflict and tension, and make the working environment extremely challenging for some.

When working towards a wellbeing-centred workplace, we must seek to create harmonious, well-working teams where differences are acknowledged, team members have the skills and capability to overcome differences, and operating as a highly functional team is expected.

As leaders we too need to be aware of how each team in our school operates and the personal cultures they contain, drawing awareness to how these may impact team culture. It can be easy to shy away from this, and not put the time or effort needed into building great teams. Instead, we might leave it to chance, assume it will happen naturally, or perceive it not to be an issue when we hear of an unhealthy team in the mix. However, if we are creating a wellbeing-centred workplace and a culture of wellbeing, every person and team matters to the overall culture, and this cannot go unnoticed or unaddressed.

Ultimately, what this means is for culture to thrive, we stop focusing on workplace culture only and instead build team cultures while developing awareness and appreciation of the personal culture each person brings.

Workplace culture

What personal and team culture attributes are evident in your workplace culture?

Overall workplace culture is a huge contributor to workplace wellbeing and, in some cases, personal wellbeing, too. Workplace culture is defined as the beliefs, norms, attitudes, values, goals and practices that characterise an organisation.

Workplace culture should not be left to chance. As leaders we can't just hope that a positive culture naturally occurs. Cultivating a positive workplace culture takes effort and dedication, but the rewards – including reducing burnout, boosting engagement, creating a sense of belonging and fuelling creativity and innovation – mean it is worth pursuing (Tobin, 2022).

A key part of developing a positive workplace culture is guiding and working with all staff to decide how you want your school to be, and then implementing actions to create the necessary change. It is not enough to have people sit in a room and list values, or create culture statements that we announce like we might communicate a change in bell times for the day or a special event that is being organised. We need to consider and involve all voices if we want staff to be engaged in creating cultural change.

While I know this may be challenging, particularly in large schools, I encourage and advocate for a designated team to begin the process and continually seek feedback from all staff along the way. Collaboration, co-design and including staff voices should never be devalued.

Managing culture also means considering the culture of the system and profession as a whole. While we can't control this, we can control how our personal, team and workplace cultures contribute to the narrative around the profession. In a time in which teaching is not seen in the most positive light at a system level, it's worth considering how our own cultures (beliefs, values and experiences) feed into this perception. Can we shift the culture of teaching as a profession by considering the role we play in creating this narrative? I think we can.

Building positive culture through values

Values symbolise our priorities and what's important to us. They vary from person to person, yet as a team and across a workplace we aim to have shared values that unite us.

In chapter 4, we looked at beliefs: how to identify and draw awareness to them and whether they are hindering or helpful. We unpacked how our beliefs shape the way we work. Values play a similar and important role in shaping wellbeing and culture.

It's not always easy to identify our values. But even if we're not conscious of them, our values influence how we invest our time, energy and finances – the three most significant assets in our lives and workplaces. The saying 'Show me what you spend your time on, and I'll show you what you value' can give you some insight into our values.

Similar to beliefs, values are not fixed; they can be altered, influenced or amplified. They also change over time based on the season of life you are in. If you are starting a new job or applying for a promotion, your top values may be things such as growth and career, whereas if you are starting a family or have young children, your top values may be family, connection or service.

To create a culture of wellbeing we need to be aware of the personal, team and workplace values that exist.

More than words

If you've been through the process of determining team or workplace values, you might recall a scenario in which you were prompted to gather around a table with your team to reflect on your core values, existing or desired. This type of exercise typically involves team members expressing words or concepts they hold important to themselves, or that they think are important for the team or workplace. You may have been asked to select words off a values list, to use values cards making it feel like a game, or to simply think of your own words.

Then, there may have been a sharing or collating of chosen words, with individuals providing explanations for this word or that and others expressing agreement or disagreement. This may have led to debates or discussions regarding the selection of the most appropriate words, especially if you were trying to select a certain number of core values from a list that might have been quite long and diverse. At the end of the process, the required number of values are determined and displayed for all team members to see. With unanimous agreement, these officially become core values.

How a workplace utilises these values varies. I've seen team and workplace values used as a reminder before beginning a meeting, or having a regular spot on the meeting agenda. I've also seen them being used to remind educators of commitments made at the start of the year, even though it is now August and the values haven't been discussed or reflected upon since January. I have seen them on posters on the wall, on websites and on school merchandise not too dissimilar from branding.

However, words alone do not suffice to foster a culture of wellbeing. If we approach values without defining them clearly, understanding their driving forces or translating them into actions, they risk remaining as fancy words on paper (or a screen) without any real impact.

While displaying values can perhaps help people to keep them front of mind, simply knowing each value is not enough to have them become part of people's shared and lived experiences. In her book *Dare to Lead*, Brené Brown (2018) says:

> *Living into our values means that we do more than profess our values, we practice them. We walk our talk – we are clear about what we believe and hold important, and we take care that our intentions, words, thoughts, and behaviours align with those beliefs.*

Without taking this next step of living into our values, they remain as words without clear, defined meaning or purpose behind them. If this is the case, no matter how great our values sound, they aren't going to support us in driving the culture of wellbeing we seek.

Defining values

A genuine value is something we actively invest in. Someone who genuinely values health will exhibit consistent habits and actions that reflect this value in their daily life. For instance, they may engage in regular exercise, prioritise mindful eating to nourish their body, seek guidance from nutritionists or personal trainers, and incorporate meditation or mindfulness into their daily routine. They may also connect health with other values that hold significance in their life, such as spending quality time with family and friends. Failure to engage in experiences such as this would reflect health be an aspiration, not a value.

Aspirations rather than values are also common in many workplaces. For example, 'respect' is listed as a core value in many workplaces, yet staff experiences, actions and behaviours can reflect the opposite: team members argue, staff engage in backsliding conversations after meetings, people are rude, deadlines aren't met and tasks are left incomplete. This is not a workplace in which the value of respect is an experience for staff.

When going through the process of defining team and workplace values, writing them down, documenting them or displaying them for everyone to see, we need to be aware that there will be varying interpretations of the values that exist. This is why we need to take our exploration of values a step further by defining them, being explicit in what they mean to us, and determining the experiences we aim to create (see figure 11). This is far more powerful than having a list of values. It pushes you to consider the impact and influence your values can have. It also allows you to observe, track and measure the culture of your workplace and the impact of your values.

Figure 11: Values as experiences

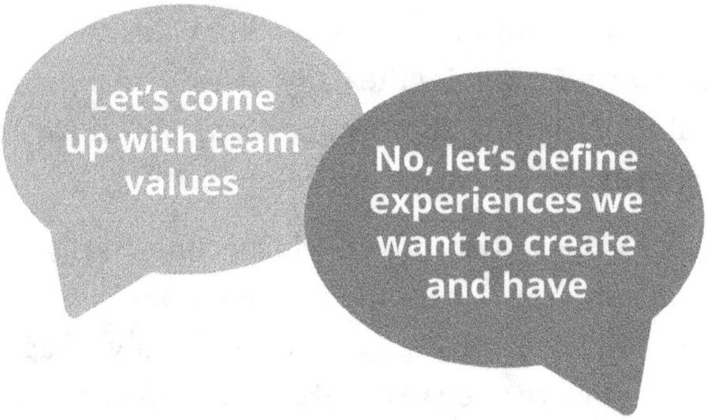

Let's come up with team values

No, let's define experiences we want to create and have

The more specific values are, the more likely they will become experiences for everyone. For example, if 'trust' is identified as a core value, it's crucial to move beyond naming the word to actively develop a shared understanding of what it means, to pinpoint daily experiences that everyone should encounter as they work together in trust, and to identify the behaviours and actions that foster trust. This in-depth articulation is essential to shift the value from being a word on paper to an integral part of the collective identity. This is why it's essential to engage in more profound, rigorous conversations that allow you to not just identify values, but reflect on and decide how those values look in day-to-day work and who you truly want to become as a workplace.

Taking values from words to experiences moves culture from something we talk about to something we experience. Naming values may seem necessary, but they alone do not require a high level of engagement. A value, without defined behaviours and actions, can easily remain an aspiration rather than a reality. Experiences, on the other hand, demand action, responsibility, commitment and effort to bring about the desired outcome.

It's highly likely you have values for your workplace, teams or even yourself, but how much time and energy do you give to discussing the language and experiences that take your values from mere aspirations to truths? How often do you do this? What does it look like? Do you simply read through your list of values at the start of a meeting to tick a box, or do you truly revisit, reflect on and question whether the values accurately reflect who you are and your experiences, actions and behaviours as a team or workplace? It's easy to say we value things such as respect, honesty, trust, communication, autonomy and flexibility, but what do these values look like in practice? Can we pinpoint the daily, weekly or ongoing behaviours, actions and habits that make these values tangible? If we can't, then we have to question whether we value our values at all.

Even though the values you choose will be universally known words, each person will bring their own interpretation and definition to them. If we don't unpack this, it can be the cause for many disagreements and challenges. This is why we need to collaboratively define values, including the experiences we want all staff to have.

It's important to move beyond surface-level value definitions and instead strive to articulate them with greater precision, debating and challenging what they truly mean in your setting. You can also take this a step further by identifying the specific experiences you intend to foster, outlining the behaviours and actions necessary to translate these values into everyday practice. This is the difference between paying lip service to values and acting with integrity in what you believe, say and do. This is what it truly means to live and breathe team and workplace values.

Table 9 provides an example of what defining values, experiences, behaviours and actions can look like.

Table 9: Values mapping

Definition	Experiences	Behaviours and actions
We value: Respect		
Valuing everyone's worth, treating them courteously and appreciating their contributions.	All team members are valued and included, regardless of their background or ideas. Mistakes are seen as opportunities for growth rather than blame.	Invite team members to share their ideas and opinions, especially if they have different viewpoints. Acknowledge and appreciate the value of diverse perspectives in decision-making. Act with kindness.
We value: Open communication		
Fostering an environment where ideas, feedback and information flow freely among team members.	Diverse perspectives are actively sought and respected in discussions. Clear and open communication is the norm.	Practise active listening by giving your full attention when someone is speaking. Avoid interrupting and wait for your turn to contribute to the discussion. Seek, give and receive feedback respectfully, even when it's hard to deliver or hear.
We value: Positive relationships		
Fostering a supportive and inclusive environment with relationships built on trust, respect and collaboration among colleagues.	Mutual support is evident, with team members assisting each other in achieving common goals.	Offer help and support to colleagues who may be facing challenges or workload issues. When giving feedback, focus on specific actions or behaviours rather than making it personal. Ensure each person is included, seen and heard.

Definition	Experiences	Behaviours and actions
We value: Engagement		
The level of involvement, enthusiasm and commitment that staff have towards their work and the workplace.	Active listening is practised, where team members genuinely pay attention to each other.	Everyone's input is encouraged and considered. Empower team members to take ownership of their tasks and projects. Show up for the work we need to do.
We value: Reliability		
Consistently delivering on commitments and meeting deadlines, and producing quality work.	Team members trust each other's competence and intentions.	Be reliable and consistent in your actions and commitments. Trust others to do their part and avoid micromanagement. Meet agreed deadlines.

This approach is significantly more impactful than simply listing the *words* as values. It creates an agreed and clear definition for all to understand. The experiences are tangible and applicable to everyone, and the behaviours and actions show what each individual is expected to do so that culture becomes part of the workplace identity. By truly stepping into this process and unpacking values in this way, using it as a means to increase expectation and accountability, wellbeing and culture have no choice but to be elevated.

Chapter summary

- Culture is made up of values, experiences, beliefs, attitudes and behaviours.
- There are three types of culture evident in a workplace: personal culture, team culture and workplace culture.
- Values underpin culture and need to be crafted together, with all staff having input.

- Values need to be unpacked to include a clear definition, experiences, behaviours and actions.
- Values, when seen as experiences, allow for impact to be measured and for accountability to occur.

From theory to action

Reflect on the culture of your workplace, and consider the following questions (you can do this yourself, with your team or as a whole staff cohort):

- What does a culture of wellbeing look like?
- How does a culture of wellbeing influence staff wellbeing?
- What are the components that make up your culture of wellbeing?
- Do all staff know and understand what a culture of wellbeing looks like in your workplace?
- What are your workplace and team values?
- What would these look like if they were experiences?
- What behaviours and actions do you need to make explicit in order for these values and experiences to become embedded?

Use the below table to map your personal, team and workplace values.

	Definition	Experiences	Behaviours and actions
Personal value			
Team value			
Workplace value			

Part 2

The How of Wellbeing Leadership

To create a workplace that values and prioritises wellbeing and considers it in decision-making, we need to focus on the four main elements of a wellbeing-centred workplace – feel well, work well, team well and lead well (see table 10) – and the characteristics that bring them together. Combined, these qualities and characteristics draw upon aspects of subjective and psychological wellbeing, align with workplace and personal wellbeing, and contribute to a positive school culture.

Table 10: Elements of a wellbeing-centred workplace

Feel well	Work well	Team well	Lead well
Feeling well is the sense of feeling positive in the workplace. It is connected to our personal wellbeing, emotional health, connection and belonging, and individual and collective resilience.	*Working well* relies on us designing how we work to support staff wellbeing. It involves asking one key question over and over again: 'Does how we work support staff wellbeing?' This is an opportunity to reimagine the systems, structures and processes that inform how we work.	*Teaming well* is often under-estimated or not even considered in discussions around staff wellbeing and culture. It's about how our teams are designed, how they're connected, how they function, and how they create collective support for wellbeing.	*Leading well* is a key driver in creating and maintaining a wellbeing-centred workplace. Leaders play a crucial role in improving staff wellbeing. Leading well means a leader takes care of their own wellbeing while also supporting others to do so.

I introduced these four elements in chapter 1, but let's break them down further:

- **Feel well:** Feeling well encompasses the emotional health of individuals, teams and the staff cohort as whole. Now more than ever we understand the impact our emotional state and ability to regulate our emotions has on our personal and professional wellbeing. Along with this are also skills to be learned in cultivating optimism, meaningful connection and building collective resilience.

- **Work well:** A workplace that prioritises staff wellbeing understands that how staff work impacts wellbeing. It's essential to get systems, structures and processes right to support productivity, engagement, and performance and growth (the three areas that make up workplace wellbeing in my teacher wellbeing framework, included in chapter 1).
- **Team well:** The teams we work in are most likely made up of the people we spend the most time with in the workplace. This means how teams are formed and function impacts wellbeing. We need to invest time into building well-functioning teams, establishing teams that work to support the overall workplace culture. We must ensure that teams are continually growing and evolving. Team functioning can make or break how individuals feel at work, as well as the collective workplace culture.
- **Lead well:** Leading well is not exclusive to those who hold a leadership role. Self-leadership is also an essential aspect of wellbeing leadership. Leadership includes how we build and grow those around us, supporting how they work. We need to be mindful that as leaders we don't fall into a space of management, devaluing the role leadership can have in workplace culture: to inspire, empower and motivate those we work with.

Along with the four elements there are eight characteristics of a wellbeing-centred workplace (see figure 12 overleaf):

1. Emotional health
2. Optimism
3. Collective resilience
4. Meaningful connection
5. Working productively
6. Engagement
7. Performance and growth
8. Psychological safety.

In part 2 of this book, we'll explore these eight characteristics in detail, discovering how they apply to the four elements and how we can work towards ensuring each of them is prevalent in our school. We'll also consider how these characteristics are influenced by or impact personal, team and workplace culture.

Figure 12: Characteristics of a wellbeing-centred workplace

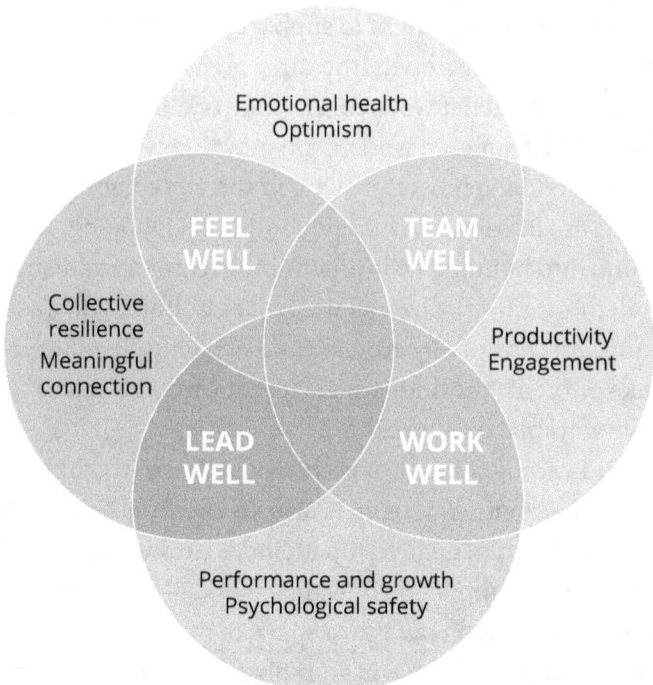

While the characteristics may seem like a lot to implement, it's important to remember that creating a new culture with staff wellbeing at the centre takes time. It's new for everyone. In some ways we are creating a new identity for who we are as leaders, educators and staff. Therefore, we need to be mindful of the internal and external shifts that need to occur before these things can become embedded.

For some time, these characteristics have been seen as the individual's responsibility to enact – for example, to regulate emotions or be resilient, to be optimists or work productively. And while individual capacity to do these things matters, so too does how we promote, facilitate and develop expectations of these within our workplaces. Individually, these skills can be developed and implemented, but without seeing them as part of a collective responsibility, we are not creating a wellbeing-centred workplace or a culture that values wellbeing.

Wellbeing leadership teaches us that it is our responsibility as leaders to consider these characteristics and build them into our dialogue, behaviours and expectations. It isn't enough just to profess them, but instead we must carefully consider how we want each of these characteristics to look and feel in our workplace. We need to believe they matter, know why they matter and put in place opportunities for each to become part of the wellbeing-centred culture we are creating. While we can't do the work of wellbeing for our staff, we can ensure characteristics such as these are valued and upheld in our teams and across the workplace.

As we move into this next part, we will explore each characteristic in terms of how it can be understood, built and applied to a workplace setting. We'll explore how you, as a leader, can model, promote and ensure expectations are built around them. We want everyone in your workplace to know this is how we do things here; this is our culture.

Chapter 6

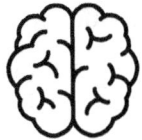

Emotional Health

I have had to learn to be okay with experiencing certain feelings. I am of the 'Suck it up, move on, no one needs to see you cry' generation. My upbringing was also filled with 'It's not that bad, just be grateful for what you've got' messaging. Repeated over many years, this led me to believe that how I felt didn't really matter, that my feelings didn't serve a purpose or have a place. I quickly learned to put on a brave face, not complain and problem-solve rather than wallow. While these tendencies no doubt contributed to who and where I am today, I missed many opportunities to develop my self-awareness, to grow and to understand who I am.

For a long time, I couldn't accurately express how I felt. I couldn't name my emotions or understand why I felt a certain way. I let my emotions control me rather than me controlling my emotions. I have had to learn to identify how I feel, and give myself permission to decide, define and draw meaning from my feelings in a way that serves me. I've had to learn to be okay with experiencing the full spectrum of emotions, understanding that how I feel is not good or bad, but an important piece of data to explore.

When we move towards a wellbeing-centred workplace, the challenge lies in building everyone's capacity to do this – to become emotionally healthy, aware and agile. A wellbeing-centred workplace requires us to build a collective culture that understands the emotional health of its people and the organisation as a whole.

In my first book, *Teacher Wellbeing*, I wrote that emotional regulation is a key component to personal wellbeing. Building on this is the notion that emotional health is a key characteristic of a wellbeing-centred workplace. By valuing emotional health and building supports for people to learn about and engage in an emotionally healthy workplace, we allow space for staff to understand how to appropriately express how they feel, build better relationships with one another, and move into proactive, solutions-focused ways of thinking. If we don't intentionally build these supports, we allow staff to exist in an emotional state that is unhelpful to themselves, others and the overall workplace culture.

As leaders we need to be acutely aware of how we model emotionally healthy strategies, support others to do the same, and set expectations for how an emotionally healthy workplace looks, feels and behaves. If we as leaders haven't built these skills for ourselves, we may struggle to do this. This is another reason why becoming self-aware and self-reflective is a key skill.

What is emotional health?

Emotional health is one aspect of mental health. It is the ability to have awareness of and cope with the whole spectrum of emotions. Emotionally healthy people have good coping mechanisms for negative emotions, and they also know when to reach out to a professional for help (DerSarkissian, 2024).

In the workplace we experience a range of emotions, and how we feel will shift across the day. We can go from calm at the start of the day to annoyed about an email, hopeful about a student learning something they have been struggling with and overwhelmed at the end of a staff meeting realising we have even more to do than we thought.

Feeling a multitude of emotions is normal; in fact, we are *supposed* to feel a range of things. However, many of us didn't go to school in a time when learning about emotions and how to manage them was part of the curriculum. Instead, we were told to suppress emotions or ignore them, or let them take us over without realising. This can mean we feel uncomfortable when we experience emotions we don't want to feel, because we don't know how to identify, process or regulate them in a healthy way.

We tend to want to categorise emotions as good or bad, positive or negative. We might feel comfortable and know what to do when we or others feel a 'positive' emotion, and uncomfortable when 'negative' emotions arise, causing us to shy away. However, no emotion or feeling is good or bad, positive or negative. Emotions and feelings simply are. They serve as data to inform us about something we are experiencing.

Understanding emotions as data allows us to be more objective with how we feel. Psychologist and neuroscientist Lisa Feldman Barrett (2018) says that our response to an experience – for example, to feel angry, sad or annoyed or to act in a certain way – is not wired into our brain, but instead made on demand, giving us more control over how we feel than we may think. This means when we are in a meeting and find ourselves becoming annoyed, we don't have to respond by shutting down, or when we are angry, we don't have to yell – we can control how we feel and the response that comes with it.

Often it is not so much how we feel that can be problematic for those we work with, but our inability to be specific about our emotions or to understand the energy and intensity each emotion carries – and how it may impact others if not thoughtfully communicated. Without this awareness, we may respond in a certain way because we think we should, because it is all we know or because we think it is acceptable. For example, it is okay to be frustrated at a decision that was made, but not okay to ignore a colleague for a number of weeks; it is okay to be angry about something that occurs in a meeting, but not okay to yell at your team and walk out. These examples highlight a response that someone may engage in because they think they have to respond that way or because they have in the past, or because they don't know another way. These responses also highlight how someone may behave if others don't question them, or hold them to a higher standard. It is time we started doing this.

Being emotionally healthy and promoting emotional health in the workplace is what's needed to ensure we can work through challenges, difficulties and differences. A lot of wellbeing issues in the workplace come from the inability to communicate well, to be open and vulnerable, and to sit in the discomfort of difficult communication. An emotionally healthy workplace does not only support staff to feel well and cultivate optimism and collective resilience, it allows staff to embrace and be open to all emotions in healthy ways. Providing structures, processes, steps and ways to describe how we feel (just as we do for students) gives us an opportunity to work together and create an emotionally healthy workplace.

Feldman Barret (2018) says that emotions are the brain's best guess for how we should feel in the moment. She says they are influenced by three things:

1. **Your body:** Your body needs to be regulated and functioning well to ensure you can respond to situations in a healthy way and control your strong emotions. This means getting enough sleep, eating well and exercising.
2. **The environment:** The environment can influence your emotions. Changing your environment can be especially useful when you feel stressed, overwhelmed, angry and so on – when this happens, go for a walk or switch to a different room.
3. **Your experiences:** Previous experiences provide a map for how we feel. This is where we need to utilise activities that bring us back to the present, for example, mindfulness and gratitude, and look for new experiences that bring us into the now.

For an emotionally healthy workplace to exist, we need to be open to talking about emotions and how we can respond to them. As leaders, we need to plan ways to support staff to do this. We also need to encourage things such as vulnerability, openness, honesty and leaning into discomfort, knowing that these build connection, trust and cohesiveness. Collectively, we need to hold each other accountable to being emotionally healthy and working through the steps to process emotions, have brave conversations and understand what it means to be emotionally healthy.

Emotional vocabulary

To build emotional health, we need to be granular with how we feel. This requires us to expand our emotional vocabulary and understand the spectrum of emotions. With many of us having a limited number of words to draw upon, building emotional vocabulary is essential for us to do. As we do with our students, actively working on this is key, and using a tool such as an emotion wheel (see figure 13) is a great way to do this. Being specific allows us to acknowledge and understand how we're feeling, meaning we can shift our responses, actions and behaviours. This helps us work towards a better understanding of ourselves and others.

Figure 13: Emotion wheel

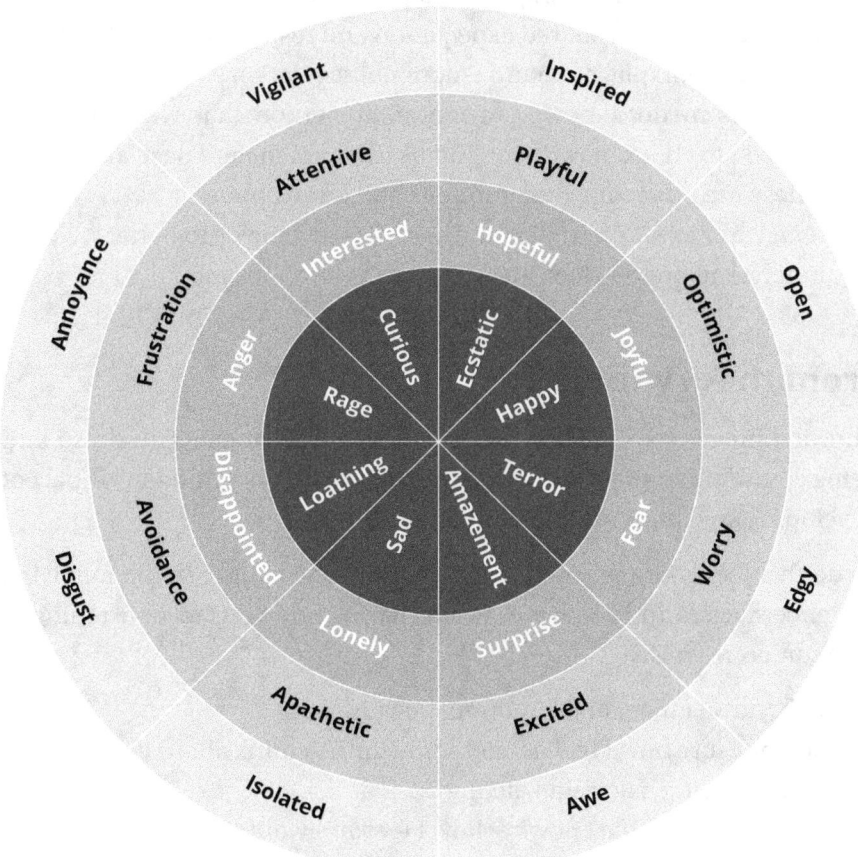

Exploring emotional states collectively allows teams and organisations to grow together. While we may each feel our own feelings, the ability to support, connect and understand how each person in our team feels builds and strengthens team connection. It allows people to know and understand each other more deeply.

Our emotional self is who we are; therefore, the emotional health of our staff, educators and teams is the emotional health of our culture.

Chapter summary

- Emotional health is our ability to understand and cope with all emotions.
- Emotionally healthy workplaces require individuals to regulate their emotions and for a shared expectation and responsibility to exist across the workplace around emotional regulation.
- Emotions are not set – we can control them more than we think.
- We need to check in with our body, environment and past, and see if these are impacting our emotions and our responses.
- Being emotionally granular and specific can help us to better understand how we feel, and how others may feel, too.

From theory to action

Knowing how to express how we feel, having the language to do so and being comfortable sharing and hearing others express emotions is part of developing an emotionally healthy workplace.

To do this, I encourage you to consider how you could use the following sentence starters and responses when sharing how you feel or listening to how someone feels:

- Right now I am feeling [emotion] because …
- I am not sure how I feel. I need some time to think about this before making a decision/acting …
- I am having trouble knowing how I feel and would like to talk about it.
- I feel [emotion] and would like some space to think.

- I'd like to feel [emotion], but I am having trouble understanding. Can you help me?
- I have some questions that I would like to ask to help me feel [emotion] about this.
- I'm not thinking clearly. I need to go for a walk [change of environment] and come back to this conversation.
- I know this is really important, but I haven't had anything to eat for a while [body]. Can you give me ten minutes so I can eat and then be in the best space to begin this work?
- I think a change of scenery could help, let's go outside [change of environment].

The following are things you can ask yourself to check in with your body, environment and past experiences:

- Am I tired/hungry/thirsty? Is that why I feel like this?
- If I slept on it, could that help?
- Should I eat before responding?
- Could a walk help me to process what I am feeling?
- Would this conversation be better held in a different room, outdoors or at a coffee shop?
- Even though I have responded like this in the past, do I need to respond like this now?
- How else can I respond to this situation? What could I do, say or ask?
- If I want x to happen next, how could I respond to ensure I help with that?
- How do I want to feel? What do I need to do to achieve this?

Here are some key questions to ask about your workplace:

- What structures exist to discuss how we feel as a team or organisation?
- How well are we using a range of emotive words in discussions where we are expressing feelings?
- Do we encourage one another to reflect on our emotional health and give space and time for this?
- How do we encourage staff to check in with their body, environment and past experiences?

Application to a wellbeing-centred workplace

Feel well	Work well	Team well	Lead well
All staff should develop skills that support emotional health, agility and regulation to help them feel well. There are two strategies everyone can utilise to do this. **Mindfulness:** Techniques such as meditation, being aware of our breath and coming back to the present can be useful here. **Walking:** A walk outside looking in the distance and scanning from left to right can create a sense of safety and calm.	Being in a calm emotional state helps us to be more productive and focused, and think more creatively. Before beginning work tasks, we want to check in with our body, environment and past experiences to ensure they are best influencing us to work well.	We need to be mindful of the emotional health of those we work with and how this may be impacting our ability to connect and collaborate as a team. An essential skill to support the emotional health of team members is to extend compassion with non-judgement. Along with this is checking in with one another, offering support and working together where possible.	As leaders we need to build and promote emotionally healthy workplaces, maintaining this as part of culture. This can be done through modelling, accountability and providing practical skill-based professional and PD.

Chapter 7

Optimism

If we are to truly create a wellbeing-centred workplace, we need to cultivate optimism. Cultivating optimism allows us to be in a space of moving forward and looking ahead, rather than getting bogged down by today or pulled back into the past. Optimism reminds us that even in the mess and the weeds, we need to remain focused on where we are going.

Optimism is essentially a mindset and one we can choose to cultivate and occupy. Being optimistic can help us engage in solution-seeking, help us accept that things are temporary (meaning they will pass), and allow us to see the opportunity in situations where others may not. To many psychologists, optimism reflects the belief that the outcomes of events or experiences will generally be positive. Others contend that optimism is more an explanatory style; it resides in the way people explain the causes of events (Psychology Today, 2023).

Optimism is said to lead to a happier life, and pessimism to lead to more stress and a feeling of dissatisfaction. Optimism can have positive impacts on our wellbeing, allowing us to flourish, while pessimism has been linked to depression and anxiety (Lonczak, 2021).

Chang (2001) notes that for those who are more naturally optimistic, the following is true:

- Optimism is a built-in trait or personality disposition.
- Optimism is directly associated with reduced depression, anxiety and stress.
- Optimistic individuals are overall healthy – both physically and emotionally.
- Optimism calls for increased resilience and coping strategies.

While some people are naturally more optimistic than others, optimism can also be taught and developed. This is called explanatory optimism. In this case, optimism is a thinking pattern rather than a part of your personality – in other words, it's a habit that can change through deliberate practice (Erickson, 2023).

Explanatory optimism is different to positive thinking. Optimism implies hope and sees us looking forward, whereas positive thinking (when used incorrectly) denies us the chance to acknowledge how we feel or what we are experiencing, instead suggesting we should just snap out of it and think happy thoughts. This way of thinking, or encouraging others to think like this, is what is known as toxic positivity. According to Cooks-Campbell (2022):

> *Toxic positivity is the pressure to only display positive emotions, suppressing any negative emotions, feelings, reactions, or experiences. It invalidates human experience and can lead to trauma, isolation, and unhealthy coping mechanisms.*

Being forced to engage in positive thinking only, especially in the workplace, can have a negative impact on wellbeing. Toxic positivity can see teams become dysfunctional as they are unable to have open conversations and support one another. It can encourage us to act with judgement rather than compassion. It also does not align with what is needed to build an emotionally healthy workplace.

The alternatives to optimism are pessimism and realism. While we are focusing on how to cultivate optimism, it is useful to understand how pessimism and realism contrast, via the following definitions (see figure 14):

- **Optimism:** Seeing the good, the positives and the opportunity in things even if the present is challenging or difficult.
- **Pessimism:** Seeing the challenges and difficulties only.
- **Realism:** Not seeing things as positive or negative, but instead being matter-of-fact about a situation.

Figure 14: Optimism, pessimism and realism

While there are certain times in which pessimism and realistic thinking are helpful, leaning towards optimism is essential to creating a wellbeing-centred workplace. Although realism is based on evidence and fact, it can limit our ability to be problem-solvers and seek solutions.

Moving from pessimistic to optimistic

We have the ability to flip from a pessimistic way of thinking to an optimistic way of thinking if we are willing to do so. Knowing how to do this is key, and it starts with awareness. So many of us are unaware of when we are adopting a pessimistic perspective. Pessimism can be a more common way of thinking when we are tired, stressed or busy, and already stretched with multiple priorities and tasks. Figure 15 (overleaf) provides a framework to use to reflect on your own thinking patterns and behaviours when working with others, and for teams.

The behaviours below the line will be present when we are in a more pessimistic state, and the behaviours above the line can shift us towards optimism. As leaders we want to encourage others to utilise what sits above the line, moving away from below-the-line behaviours.

Figure 15: Moving from pessimism towards optimism

choice	patience	hope	**OPTIMISTIC**
accountable	action	acceptance	
ownership	solution-focused	responsibility	
punish	denial	procrastination	**PESSIMISTIC**
problem-focused	negativity	justification	
defensiveness	blame	excuses	

How to build learned optimism in schools

Cultivating optimism is a collective effort that can become an inherent way of thinking if it's built into conversations, meetings and strategic planning. As leaders, it is our responsibility to motivate and inspire those we lead in ways that cultivate optimism.

To cultivate optimism, we need to understand the idea of learned optimism: a concept that says when we recognise our negative self-talk, beliefs, assumptions and ways of thinking, we can change our behaviours, actions and attitudes to be more positive.

Knowing some people are more optimistic than others, and that this can have a significant impact on wellbeing and culture, we want to be able to create a workplace that values and promotes learned optimism. To do this well, we also need to understand what may get in the way of this: that is, learned helplessness (see table 11).

Learned helplessness is the opposite of learned optimism, and can be the difference between someone moving forward or staying stagnant where they are. Learned helplessness can see someone sit in a space of excuse-making and not knowing what to do, but also lacking motivation to see other options and move forward. Despite its drawbacks, learned helplessness has many benefits. It requires no responsibility, action, risk-taking or innovation. In fact, it is the perfect strategy to engage in if you want things to remain the same, comfortable, and as they have always been (which, in schools, is a common way of thinking).

Table 11: The difference between learned helplessness and learned optimism

Learned helplessness	Learned optimism
No responsibility required	Responsibility taken
Focus on what they can't control	Focus on what can be controlled
Negative self-talk	Positive self-talk
Giving up when things are challenging	Drive and determination
Focusing on the negative	Looks for solutions

We want to be utilising ways to build optimism and ensure our staff and teams know how to do so. This will create a culture where collectively we are always moving forward and not being dragged down by perceived problems or challenges. In a school setting, the latter is all too common; we focus too much on the work piling up, how many books we have to mark, the meetings we need to have or lessons we need to plan. When we sit in a space of learned helplessness and put our energy into this way of thinking and being, it leaves very little room for learned optimism to come into play – and optimism is by far a better use of our time and energy, individually and collectively.

The three Ps of optimism

I recommend utilising Martin Seligman's three Ps of optimism when helping teams and individuals to move away from the doom-and-gloom thinking of learned helplessness (Seligman, 2006). This tool can take people from a place of feeling stuck and thinking negatively and narrowly to a place of seeing opportunities, thinking in hopeful ways and engaging strategically.

The three Ps of optimism are:

- **Personalisation:** This is how individuals attribute the causes of events in their lives. Optimistic people tend to attribute positive events to their own actions and abilities, while attributing negative events to external factors that are temporary or situational. This perspective fosters a sense of empowerment and control over experiences, circumstances and what can be done next.
- **Pervasiveness:** This relates to how an individual perceives an event impacting other areas of their life, and whether it is positive or negative. Optimistic people tend to see setbacks as specific to particular situations and not as pervasive across all aspects of their lives. They recognise that a setback in one area does not necessarily mean failure in all areas.
- **Permanence:** This refers to the belief about the duration of events, whether they are temporary or long-lasting. Optimistic people tend to see positive events as enduring and negative events as temporary and transient. This perspective helps them maintain hope and resilience in the face of challenges, knowing that difficulties are not permanent and that better things lie ahead.

Let's take a look at how to apply this in the workplace by considering a range of unhelpful assumptions, and how we can transform these into helpful assumptions. This is a beneficial skill for personal life and wellbeing, but also for a wellbeing-centred workplace (see table 12).

Table 12: Applying the three Ps in the workplace

Unhelpful assumptions (learned helplessness)	Helpful assumptions (learned optimism)
Personalisation	
I didn't get promoted because my boss doesn't like me.	I didn't get promoted, but I understand that my boss's decision is likely based on factors beyond personal feelings, such as my qualifications and fit for the role.
When my work colleague gives me a hard time it's because they are trying to make me look bad.	When my work colleague gives me a hard time, I recognise that they might have different perspectives or priorities. It's not necessarily about making me look bad, but rather about addressing issues or improving our work.

Unhelpful assumptions *(learned helplessness)*	Helpful assumptions *(learned optimism)*
I didn't get a 'thank you' from my leader because they don't value me.	I didn't get a 'thank you' from my leader, but I know they appreciate my contributions. Recognition can come in various forms, and I trust that my efforts are valued within the team.

Pervasiveness

Unhelpful assumptions	Helpful assumptions
My team didn't like my idea, so now I'm convinced I suck at my job altogether.	My team didn't like my idea, but I understand that it's just one aspect of my job. It doesn't mean I'm incompetent overall; there are many other areas where I excel and contribute.
I said the wrong thing to a parent, and now I'm worried I'm not going to be able to talk to any parents.	I said the wrong thing to a parent, but I know that communication can be challenging at times. It's a specific incident, and I can learn from it to improve my interactions with parents in the future.
That lesson flopped, I'll never teach that concept again.	That lesson didn't go as planned, but it's an opportunity to reassess and refine my teaching strategies. It doesn't mean I'll never be able to teach that concept again; I can adapt and try different approaches to ensure better outcomes next time.

Permanence

Unhelpful assumptions	Helpful assumptions
I didn't get the promotion, and now I'll never get a leadership position.	I didn't get the promotion this time, but I understand that opportunities for leadership positions can arise in the future based on my continued growth and contributions.
The lesson failed, and now I'm convinced I'm always going to be a failure.	The lesson didn't go as planned, but I know that failure is part of the learning process. It doesn't define my ability to succeed in future endeavours.
I missed the deadline for reports. I'll always be behind schedule.	I missed the deadline for reports, but I recognise that it's a temporary setback. By improving my time-management skills and learning from this experience, I can ensure that I meet deadlines in the future.

The nuances of optimism

The challenge when working with optimism, pessimism and realism is knowing when to draw upon each way of thinking. It's about understanding how a particular perspective and way of thinking makes you feel and impacts your energy, and whether it adds to or detracts from your overall wellbeing. This is especially true in teams when we're working together to engage in optimistic or pessimistic thinking. That said, while pessimism may at times serve a purpose, for the most part we want to cultivate optimism to give us hope for the future, and also use it to design and create the change we seek.

Cultivating optimism does not lie with one person. It is everyone's responsibility to bring about ways of thinking that support cultivating optimism. This may mean drawing attention to where energy is focused in a meeting, asking a question to get everyone to think differently or sharing a different perspective. Cultivating optimism requires collective responsibility to impact a wellbeing-centred workplace. As leaders, it is our responsibility to ensure we know when and how to cultivate optimism, and to build others' resources so they can do so for themselves, and within their teams.

Chapter summary

- Optimism is essentially a mindset and one we can choose to cultivate and engage in.
- Optimism can occur more naturally in some people, yet others can learn optimistic ways of thinking.
- Those with more optimism are healthier, less stressed, and have better wellbeing overall.
- Optimism can help us find solutions to problems or challenges.
- Cultivating optimism allows us to actively work on being solutions-focused despite things being challenging in the present.

From theory to action

Cultivating optimism

The following questions can help you and your team gauge how optimism and pessimism are working in your team:

- What is our most common collective perception: optimistic or pessimistic?
- How can we cultivate more optimism?
- When do we need to draw upon pessimistic thinking?

The following questions can help you to cultivate optimism. These questions should drive curiosity along with hope, and bring about vuja de – the act of facing something familiar, but seeing it with a fresh perspective that enables us to gain new insights into old problems.

You can use these questions for yourself or with your team:

- While this may be a problem right now, what are some of the solutions for next time?
- What choices do we have so we can move forward?
- Are there any other solutions we haven't considered but should?
- Who is going to take action on this?
- What do we need to do to change this? How will we do so?

Other ways to cultivate optimism include promoting an environment where staff are encouraged to be brave, courageous and vulnerable in the possibilities they suggest and ideas they have for the future. To do this, try using the following questions and prompts:

- If you could do anything at all right now with this situation, what would it be?
- What, if anything, would you like to start doing?
- What, if anything, would you like to stop doing?
- What crazy ideas do you have, no matter whether they seem possible or not?

Moving from learned helplessness to learned optimism

Utilise the scaffold overleaf to take your staff and team through a process to help them move from unhelpful thinking to helpful thinking.

	Unhelpful thinking *(learned helplessness)*	**Helpful thinking** *(learned optimism)*
Personalisation		
Pervasiveness		
Permanence		

Application to a wellbeing-centred workplace

Feel well	Work well	Team well	Lead well
Become aware of your own self-talk, paying attention to whether this is creating an optimistic or pessimistic way of thinking. If your thinking is limiting optimism, see if you can shift this by using the three Ps framework.	We need to cultivate optimism to promote productivity and engagement. Exploring learned helplessness and learned optimism will ensure we can work well and look for solutions.	As a team we need to be aware of how our collective optimism or pessimism influences our team culture and how we work. This means coming together to utilise questioning techniques that help to challenge and shift thinking and perspective when we're feeling stuck or challenged.	As leaders we may find ourselves in the space of pessimistic thinking more than optimistic thinking as our colleagues come to us with challenges and obstacles. We need to be aware of what may be impacting this type of thinking, and how we can compassionately support and guide others to a more optimistic way of thinking.

Chapter 8

Collective Resilience

Resilience is a key part of my teacher wellbeing framework I introduced in chapter 1. As educators, we tend we teach students about resilience while not necessarily having built it within ourselves.

Most of us think of resilience in terms of how we bounce back from a setback, but it is far more than this. As with all of the strategies I discuss in this book, building resilience requires self-awareness, self-compassion and self-acceptance.

We may consider resilience as something we only need when we are facing adversity or a challenge. But the truth is, we need to be resilient and engaging in adaptive coping strategies every day. Resilience is needed for both big and small occurrences: from receiving an email from a parent to finding out your teacher BFF is moving schools. While the intensity of these experiences is not the same, they still require resilience so we can be aware of the event and our emotional state, engage in adaptive coping strategies, make conscious decisions and take meaningful action.

We can draw upon these steps individually and engage in them independently of others, but building collective resilience requires us to band together and actively engage in healthy resilience strategies that support everyone. Collective resilience is defined as: 'The ability of human beings to adapt and collectively cope with crises in adversity' (Liu et al., 2022).

As leaders of staff wellbeing, we are aiming to build and draw upon our staff members' individual resilience to ensure teams and the entire workplace band together to harness their collective efficacy. As it is inevitable to go through phases of change, challenge and growth, we want our teams and staff groups to have skills and strategies to support each other to adapt in healthy ways.

Adapting is a characteristic of high resilience. The American Psychological Association (2020) defines resilience as 'the process of adapting well in the face of trauma or tragedy, threats or other significant sources of stress'. There is no denying that collective resilience is needed in the world, especially in schools, given the need to adapt to sources of stress. Teaching is stressful, working in a school is stressful, and right now in our industry there are many additional stressors to overcome such as teacher shortages, increasing student needs and the new curriculum.

With these changes and circumstances being applicable to everyone – not unique to an individual person, team or school – collective resilience needs to become a resource we all draw upon. We must come together not just to get through these current times, but to ensure we are able to learn and grow together.

For this to happen we first need to be aware of how we may be coping as a collective, in teams and across the workplace, and understand how this relates to both subjective and psychological wellbeing (see table 13).

As a team or workplace we sometimes need to engage in quick fixes simply to boost our mood, but we also need to engage in long-term strategies to build and continually improve our resilience. Collectively, we need to be mindful of the fact that the strategies we use are either adaptive (resourceful) or maladaptive (unresourceful). It can be helpful to think of it like this: our adaptive coping strategies are positive, work for us and are resourceful – they help our team and workplace move forward; our maladaptive coping strategies are sometimes negative, work against us and are unhelpful – they keep our teams and workplaces stuck and don't help us grow. While a coffee van is great, it doesn't reduce stress or address the stress at its root cause.

If we want to create a wellbeing-centred workplace that is growing, healthy and supportive, we need to ensure our resilience strategies are adaptive. At times, we may see individuals, teams or everyone dip into a maladaptive space, and while this may be understandable, we want to ensure we support our teams and staff to move as quickly as possible into an adaptive space. This is important not just for how we cope, but as it also relates to cultivating optimism.

Table 13: Workplace and team adaptive and maladaptive strategies for subjective and psychological wellbeing

	Subjective wellbeing *(Quick fixes based on seeking pleasure or avoiding pain.)*	**Psychological wellbeing** *(Long-term strategies based on fulfilment, meaning and purpose.)*
Adaptive (resourceful) coping strategies	Morning teas Cancelled meetings Venting to colleagues Chocolate in the staffroom Coffee van in week ten	Utilising strategies to cultivate optimism Reframing negative thoughts Reflecting on failure Setting new goals and creating strategic plans for success
Maladaptive (unresourceful) coping strategies	Gossiping Procrastination Work avoidance Making excuses or justifying the why or how	Disengagement Negative spiral from one thing to another (looping) Continually not taking responsibility for what you can control and do Always being problem-focused

If we allow maladaptive strategies to become our default, we run the risk of having negativity and learned helplessness creep through our workplace faster than chickenpox spreads in a prep classroom. We don't want this for one crucial reason: when we're in this space, anxiety and stress increase, and, even though we may see these as individual traits, stress and anxiety are contagious. This phenomenon is known as emotional contagion and it's another reason to build emotional health and cultivate optimism. Research has shown it's possible to 'catch' the emotions of others, including in the workplace, as we naturally (and unconsciously) mimic the behaviours of those we spend a lot of time with (Wilding, 2021).

As we can see from table 13, many of our psychological strategies are affected by our emotions – gossip, procrastination, being caught in a negative spiral or always focusing on the problem. For this reason, to create a culture where collective resilience is the default, we cannot let anxiety, stress, doubt or fear percolate. Once they are in, they are hard to wind back.

How to build collective resilience

As we look to build a wellbeing-centred workplace where staff wellbeing informs decision-making and drives change, we need to draw upon collective resilience to navigate the unknown. There is no doubt that any change process or new initiative in a workplace requires staff to be resilient, and the same applies when introducing a wellbeing-related initiative. There is work to do. Some of the changes may be easy and quick to implement with the impact noticed almost immediately, whereas other initiatives may take longer and feel harder, with the impact taking time to come to fruition. This is where collective resilience will come into play.

The strength of collective resilience within your teams and across the workplace is influenced by each individual's personal resilience strategies, along with the dynamics, relationships, team morale and cohesiveness of each team and the workplace as a whole. It is not as simple as assuming your own personal resilience strategies are enough to see your team build great collective resilience. Collective resilience, just like culture, needs to be well-designed, curated and supported.

There are three steps that help to bring about resilient thinking as we work through various obstacles and challenges, either as part of our wellbeing strategy, in our day-to-day functioning as we work, or as we go through a significant phase of change. These three steps are rethink, reimagine and redesign.

Rethink

Rethinking requires us to rethink our current situation and draw upon a new perspective. Collectively, we need to draw upon all perspectives, ensuring we all agree and understand the situation we are focusing on.

Sometimes, as we learned in chapter 7, our own thinking and perspectives can impact our resilience. Rethinking as a group gives us the chance to establish collective meaning so everyone can move on to reimagine.

Reimagine

Reimagining is an opportunity to think about what could be. Collective resilience requires the ability for all to speak up, share ideas and offer insights. Reimagining helps us avoid getting stuck by the problem or obstacle, instead drawing upon some vuja de thinking.

When we reimagine, we are strengthening our collective resilience by supporting one another to ensure we make sense of a situation or challenge without letting our own mindset or perspectives stop us from moving forward. The ability to work through problems collectively not only sees us find solutions more quickly, but also supports each person's experience with the intent of moving forward.

Redesign

The redesign phase sees us put into action what we have collectively reimagined. We are redesigning our approach and strategy to change. Collectively we are strengthening action by having multiple hands create change.

This again highlights how collective resilience can become part of a collective support strategy as well as encouraging innovative and creative thinking.

While there may be parallels between the reimagine and redesign phases, here we are drawing upon collective resilience to act and begin taking meaningful, strategic and visible steps to move forward.

Use the questions outlined in table 14 to support the implementation of these three steps to build collective resilience.

Table 14: Rethink, reimagine and redesign: questions for each phase

Phase	Questions
Rethink	What do we know about the obstacle or challenge?
	What is true? What isn't true?
	What are the positives?
	What are the negatives?
	What is the most important thing to note?
Reimagine	What are some solutions?
	What are some things we haven't thought of?
	If anything was possible, what would you like to do?
	Who has an idea you find inspiring?
	Which idea excites us the most?
Redesign	What is actually possible?
	What is the best thing to do right now?
	How can we support one another to do this?
	What do we need to get started?
	When can we start?
	What is the first step to take action?

When we build collective resilience, what we are aiming for is to develop a culture that is stable, strong and connected, with the ability to support, challenge and encourage each person to grow through any moment of challenge, big or small. By understanding resilience as a collective effort, we remove the notion that it is one person's job to fix, or one person's challenge to overcome. No matter what our team or workplace is facing, it impacts all of us, and the more we can foster collective resilience, the more we will work on sustainable change that supports everyone, which improves wellbeing and culture.

Chapter summary

- Collective resilience is the resilience a group has and utilises when faced with obstacles. It is not just the result of individual resilience, but how the group works together.
- Collective resilience needs to be built via adaptive coping strategies.
- The process of rethinking, reimagining and redesigning encourages collective resilience.
- Collective maladaptive resilience strategies can induce stress and anxiety, which are contagious.
- Our emotions impact our ability to be resilient.

From theory to action

Reflecting on your workplace, ask these questions:

- Have we spent time establishing collective resilience?
- What are our collective resilience strategies or steps?
- Do we follow the rethink, reimagine, redesign steps, or similar?

Think of a challenge or obstacle you, your team or your workplace are facing. Use the rethink, reimagine and redesign steps to plan a strategic approach using the table below:

Current challenge:		
Phase	Questions	Answers
Rethink	What do we know about the obstacle or challenge?	
	What is true? What isn't true?	
	What are the positives?	
	What are the negatives?	
	What is the most important thing to note?	

Phase	Questions	Answers
Reimagine	What are some solutions?	
	What are some things we haven't thought of?	
	If anything was possible, what would you like to do?	
	Who has an idea you find inspiring?	
	Which idea excites us the most?	
Redesign	What is actually possible?	
	What is the best thing to do right now?	
	How can we support one another to do this?	
	What do we need to get started?	
	When can we start?	
	What is the first step to take action?	

Application to a wellbeing-centred workplace

Feel well	Work well	Team well	Lead well
Resilience is higher when we have adequate sleep, eat well, move our body and self-regulate. Individually we need to utilise these things to feel well and boost resilience.	When working through challenging tasks requiring grit and perseverance, we need to utilise collective resilience. This requires us to bring attention to our coping strategies, moving them from maladaptive to adaptive.	As a team it is vital to use rethink, reimagine and redesign as a tool to build collective resilience. We also need to hold each other accountable to this to ensure team culture remains proactive and positive, being aware of emotional contagion.	As leaders we need to model resilience showing we consistently do this across the school environment. We need to support adaptive coping strategies and the use of the rethink, reimagine and redesign tool.

Chapter 9

Meaningful Connection

It is common to cite positive relationships as the essential component to building a collaborative and cohesive staff cohort with high levels of wellbeing. What we often overlook is *how* this happens – the ways we can support connection to flourish.

Without considering *how* we connect or finding ways to connect meaningfully, our staff may connect only in transactional, meaningless ways. This can result in relationships that appear pleasant on the surface, but aren't meaningful or deeply established to support how we collaborate and work. This ultimately impacts how we engage with one another and how we work together. The *how* (what we do to connect) is just as important as the *why* (to work and team well).

The how of meaningful connection

Have you ever wondered why staff don't feel connected, yet seem to have a connection? It is often because the connections that do exist are transactional or surface-level, rather than the deep, meaningful connections based on a collective or shared purpose.

In *Together: The Healing Power of Human Connection in a Sometimes Lonely World*, Vivek Murthy (2020), US Surgeon General describes three types of loneliness: intimate, relational and collective. These types of loneliness relate to how we connect in the workplace (see table 15).

Table 15: Loneliness and meaningful connection in the workplace
Adapted from Murthy, 2020.

Type of loneliness as described by Murthy (2020)	How this relates to meaningful connection in the workplace
Intimate (or emotional) loneliness: longing for a close confidante or intimate partner, sharing a mutual bond and trust	Do all staff have an opportunity to build connections with colleagues that align with similar feelings and interests, creating a space of support and trust?
Relational (or social) loneliness: longing for quality friendships and social support	Do all staff receive social support in relation to how they work, their workload and when they are experiencing stress?
Collective loneliness: hunger for a network or community of people who share your sense of purpose and interests	Do all staff have the opportunity to exist in groups across the workplace that are outside their year/subject/core role, which align to a shared interest, in order to enhance their sense of purpose?

If you look around at your school, you may now see that not all connections are meaningful, and perhaps also that not all relationships are built on meaningful connections. Given a school is significantly busy and fast-moving, we can easily neglect the need to foster meaningful connections. When we become too busy, pulled in multiple directions, we feel like we don't have time for one another, despite valuing the relationships we aim to have.

When this occurs, our connections become meaningless, transactional and focused on tasks rather than relationships. We find ourselves connecting only when we need something or when a deadline is nearing, or if we are feeling the pressure of day-to-day tasks and need assistance. We don't take time to engage in meaningful connection. We don't ask how our colleagues are with the intention to really listen. We don't connect with groups that exist beyond our classroom, offices or area of work. We don't have the capacity to stay connected with one another or support each other through times of stress or intense workload, as we are too busy trying to survive ourselves.

So the question is: how do we ensure we foster meaningful connection points as a way to build positive relationships, and not assume all relationships are positive or purposeful just because they exist?

The key to this is to consider why we are connecting, knowing that the purpose of doing so is ultimately to improve workplace wellbeing including how we feel at work, how we work, and how we grow as an organisation. Connection in the workplace is not solely done to get to know one another, but ultimately to enhance our working environment and working relationships. If we are only focusing on developing positive relationships through more relaxed and social opportunities to connect, we are missing valuable opportunities to understand that all connections can and should be considered as a way to contribute to positive relationships in the workplace. This includes team meetings, staff meetings, and professional conversations including feedback and accountability.

The problem is, we perceive positive relationships to only be built on connections that create a positive emotion. Yet, as we have learned, emotional health and being able to manage both positive and negative emotions are part of a healthy, wellbeing-centred workplace. The misconception here is that anything that is seen as negative cannot be a contributing factor to a positive relationship.

What is interesting about this is that positive relationships in the workplace are said to be based on relationships that have trust, connection, support and honesty. This means not shying away from conversations, meetings or topics that may be challenging or perceived as negative, but seeing them as something in which everyone has the emotional health, both individually and collectively, to manage. In this way we engage in meaningful connection that supports us to feel and work well.

Honesty, openness and vulnerability, which at times may be uncomfortable, are not negative. Conversations or connections that require these things do not detract from our wellbeing, but instead increase it. What we think meaningful connection at work involves is often very different from the reality of what makes a connection deep and significant (see figure 16).

Figure 16: Meaningful connection at work

What we think meaningful connection at work involves	What it also involves
Morning teas	Open, honest dialogue
After-work social activities	Vulnerable conversations
Friday drinks	Planned, intentional time to meet and collaborate
Birthday clubs	Giving and receiving feedback

POSITIVE RELATIONSHIPS

Gathering versus connection

Part of connecting meaningfully to support workplace wellbeing is understanding that how we connect should improve our productivity, engagement, performance and growth.

In *The Art of Gathering: How We Meet and Why it Matters*, author Priya Parker (2018) encourages us to consider the purpose of each gathering and why we are doing so. She says: 'When we don't examine the deeper assumptions behind why we gather, we end up skipping too quickly to replicating old, staid formats of gathering.'

In schools, there simply isn't an infinite amount of time, yet we can always find a reason for a meeting. To prioritise wellbeing and meaningful connection, we must consider the reasons we gather: for what purpose, and whether the meeting is meaningful or simply something we have always done. If you were to consider all the gatherings across your workplace, do they have reason, a clear purpose, functionality and meaning?

This is yet another opportunity to truly begin to consider how our schools are designed, how they function, and whether purpose and wellbeing underpins how we work.

When we confuse gathering with connection, we create ways for people to come together that are not in line with how or why we connect. Just because we are gathering doesn't mean we are connecting. What is needed is to gather on purpose, so meaningful connection can occur.

To challenge how we gather and to build opportunities for meaningful connection, Parker (2022) created *The New Rules of Gathering: A Guide to Planning with Purpose for Any Occasion* (available for free on her website). In it she shares five rules to consider when planning a gathering:

1. Give your gathering a purpose
2. Make purpose your bouncer
3. Design your invitation to persuade
4. Ditch etiquette for rules
5. Close with intention.

Let's take a look at how these rules can help us establish meaningful connections in our schools to support a wellbeing-centred workplace (in short, how do we stop meeting for meeting's sake and be more intentional when we do gather?). See table 16 overleaf.

Designing meaningful connections cannot be left to chance. It requires intentional, well-thought-out opportunities to connect, meaning we need to design our meetings for the connection we are wanting to cultivate. The connections we want and need in our schools should not be described as 'transactional' or 'task oriented', yet in my experience, transaction and task is what often drives gathering and connection in schools. A meeting should be an opportunity for meaningful connection. When we meet too often or our meetings lack purpose and structure, we waste time, creating disengaged, uninterested staff. It also adds to stress and creates meaningless connection, which does not support a wellbeing-centred workplace.

Table 16: Rules for gathering in schools
Adapted from Parker, 2022.

What this means	What this commonly looks like in schools	How this can look in schools
Rule 1: Give your gathering a purpose		
The gathering needs a reason. The more specific you are, the more effective it is. This helps to know what goes on the agenda and what doesn't.	Meetings for meeting's sake. Meeting because we always have. Task-driven agendas with no specific purpose. One person leading the meeting.	Know why you are at a meeting. Be clear and specific; 'Team Meeting' is not a purpose. Focus on what is needed, not what is normally done. Consider who is best to organise and plan the meeting. Have each attendee draw upon their strengths in the meeting.
Rule 2: Make purpose your bouncer		
You purpose drives what goes in and what stays out of your meeting. This includes agenda items and who is invited to attend the meeting. Including all the possible people and agenda items can detract from the purpose.	Random, disconnected agenda items. Surprise and last-minute items being added to the agenda. Anything and anyone is welcome. Time wasted due to not following or sticking to a purpose. Thinking everything matters equally, not being able to slow down, pause or stop the discussion.	Consider who needs to be at the meeting and why. Just because they are in the team does not mean they need to be there. Stay true to the purpose of the meeting by reducing the number of people and/or items on the agenda. To cultivate meaningful action from those in the meeting, stick to the purpose (yes, there is a lot going on, but getting distracted can reduce engagement).
Rule 3: Design your invitation to persuade		
An invite to a meeting (even if it is recurring) is the beginning of the meeting. The invite should prepare people and tell them what to expect. The invite should also encourage people to prepare, so they know what to bring and what they will need. This sets the tone for the meeting.	No agenda included in the invite, or a limited agenda only. People not knowing how to prepare or what to bring. People unaware of the mindset or mental state they need to bring to the meeting, which means they are caught off guard, resulting in an unproductive meeting. (For example, for some people, creativity cannot be turned on instantly; instead they need time to ponder.)	Be specific about why the meeting is occurring including what will be discussed, why and by whom. Outline how you want people to be when they attend the meeting. For example, do they need to be curious and ready to ask questions, think creatively about solutions to a problem, or ready to focus and get things done? Remind people that the reason for the meeting is the identified purpose (focus on the why, not the what) and that this will be adhered to (even though there may be other pressing items).

What this means	What this commonly looks like in schools	How this can look in schools
Rule 4: Ditch etiquette for rules		
Creating playful, pop-up rules adds more fun (which we all need). Pop-up rules often go against etiquette. People connect and bond in new ways.	We begin the year creating team norms or something similar. We focus on uniform behaviours linked to professionalism. We don't consider connection within team norms.	Consider pop-up rules that can be used in meetings. For example, no talking about specific students, no going off track with 'just one other thing', or something completely different such as not using acronyms (because we know schools love an acronym). Design pop-up rules that help people to be more present or that ask people to avoid group behaviours that are unhelpful and distracting. Encourage humour and playfulness, suggesting penalties for breaking the pop-up rule such as doing someone's duty or being on staffroom clean-up. Share the role of pop-up rule creator around.
Rule 5: Close with intention		
Endings matter; they influence feelings, meaning, ideas and memories. An ending should revisit the purpose. It should also give people an opportunity to make sense of why you met in the first place.	Meeting ends are rushed or non-existent. We use the bell as the signal that the meeting is over rather than whether we have achieved our purpose. We don't revisit the purpose of the meeting (because we most likely didn't have one). Any agenda items we didn't have time for (again, because meetings lack purpose and intention) are pushed to next week, sent as an email or deemed not important.	Don't rush the end of a meeting. Keep an eye on the time and allow time and space for an intentional meeting end to occur. Revisit the purpose of the meeting with everyone reflecting on whether it has been achieved. Consider introducing a token to show the meeting has ended, making the meeting more memorable – such as a moment of gratitude or an opportunity to share how we feel (a great way to link in emotional health).

Chapter summary

- Positive relationships are built on meaningful connections.
- Just because we are meeting, doesn't mean it is purposeful or meaningful.
- We often overlook ways to connect meaningfully and need to intentionally design these.
- Positive relationships in the workplace help us to be engaged, productive, and perform and grow together.
- Positive relationships can still exist even when we are connecting in ways that are uncomfortable (such as within vulnerable, honest, brave conversations).

From theory to action

Ask yourself and your teams the following questions:

- Do we consider how meaningful connections can occur?
- Are opportunities for meaningful connection both formal and informal?
- Are meetings created around purpose?

Review all current meetings

Using the table opposite, reflect on the rules of gathering from Parker (2022). You can repeat this exercise with all staff, or by thinking of all the meetings that exist in your workplace.

Questions to ask	Your answers	Room for improvement
Rule 1: Give your gathering a purpose What is the reason for this gathering? Can you be more specific?		
Rule 2: Make purpose your bouncer What is usually on the agenda? Who usually attends? Do these align or detract from the purpose?		
Rule 3: Design your invitation to persuade Do you have an invite for this meeting? If so, does it prepare people and tell them what to expect? Does it set the tone for the meeting? Does it help people to know what to prepare and bring?		
Rule 4: Ditch etiquette for rules What, if any, are your pop-up rules? What pop-up rules could you introduce to help people bond in new ways?		
Rule 5: Close with intention Do you have an end to the meeting that influences feelings, meaning, ideas and memories? Does the ending revisit the purpose, bringing the gathering together?		

Application to a wellbeing-centred workplace

Feel well	Work well	Team well	Lead well
Bringing awareness to our emotional health will help us connect and build better relationships with those around us. It is important to recognise how we may be feeling and how this impacts our connections with others.	The better we connect with and know our staff, the more likely we are to work well together, being more productive and engaged in the work we do. Therefore, we need to value and make time for connection to help us work well.	In teams we need to bring about connection before content. This means knowing those in our teams on a personal level so we can understand who they are, what they bring to the team, and how we can support one another.	As leaders we need to offer ways for staff to meaningfully connect, as well as consider when we connect. We want to provide opportunities for staff to connect and build positive relationships outside of 'working', as well as create structures and purposeful reasons for connecting.

Chapter 10

Working Productively

Feeling productive is a key indicator of high workplace wellbeing. When people are exhausted physically, emotionally and mentally, they are not able to focus on the things that matter and that add value, nor can they connect meaningfully with their colleagues. Exhausted people don't have the bandwidth to care or contribute to their full potential (Deutscher, 2023).

It's essential we start to see productivity as a key area to develop to enhance the wellbeing of staff. Too often we underestimate how we do things, the systems, structures and processes, not knowing why we aren't as productive as we would like, finding ourselves doing things the way they have always been done without reflecting on the efficiency or effectiveness of the tasks we are doing. We also neglect to take into account other factors that contribute to how productive individuals and teams may be, from physical health to team dysfunctionality – all of these things impact productivity and therefore workplace wellbeing.

As leaders it is essential we understand all components that contribute to workplace productivity so we can intentionally design ways of working that allow for the best possible opportunity for staff to work well, while also taking into account the what, why and how of productivity.

Contributors to productivity

As shown in figure 17, there are three interconnected elements that together contribute to an individual or team's ability to be productive:

- The three Es of productivity
- Workplace operations
- Overall factors.

Figure 17: Contributors to productivity

THE 3 Es OF PRODUCTIVITY
Efficiency
Effectiveness
Energetic sustainability

Contributors to productivity

WORKPLACE OPERATIONS
Systems
Structures
Processes

OVERALL FACTORS
Job and workplace
Personal factors
Mental and physical health factors

As we can see, productivity is not solely the result of one particular factor: for example, time management, high job demands or inefficient systems. Knowing that productivity relies on multiple contributing factors spanning from the personal (such as health) to workplace specifics (such as systems), we can see why individual and collective responsibility for personal and workplace wellbeing is required to create a productive, wellbeing-centred workplace.

The three Es of productivity

Productivity is often thought of as how fast we complete a task compared with how much effort we put in. We feel productive when we do more than anticipated in a given amount of time, or when we complete tasks more quickly than we thought. Ultimately, we connect productivity to time, effort and achievement.

I believe productivity results from the following three factors (see figure 18 overleaf):

- **Efficiency:** Efficiency means utilising our resources well. It takes into account the time and pace at which we get something done. If we are working efficiently, we are maximising output while minimising waste, ensuring tasks are completed in a timely manner. If a task takes longer than we perceive it should to complete, we can find ourselves resenting the task and feeling unfulfilled by the work we are doing.
- **Effectiveness:** Effectiveness means achieving goals or outcomes in a way that meets expectations and standards. It's about getting things done well, to an agreed standard, and making sure things are completed with the desired impact and purpose. If we are completing tasks but don't understand why or can't see the value in what we are doing, we can become disengaged and even do the bare minimum required just to get things done.
- **Energetic sustainability:** Energetic sustainability means managing our energy levels to sustain productivity without feeling depleted or running on empty after completing tasks. It involves maintaining a balance between expending energy on tasks and replenishing energy by doing things such as taking short breaks or breaking large tasks into small chunks. Without this approach, we may find we can't perform at our best. This may even be the reason for experiencing increased long-term stress and exhaustion.

If we fail to prioritise the three Es, our productivity slows down. Therefore, we must consider how work tasks are designed, completed and allocated to ensure productivity occurs through working efficiently, effectively and in energetically sustainable ways.

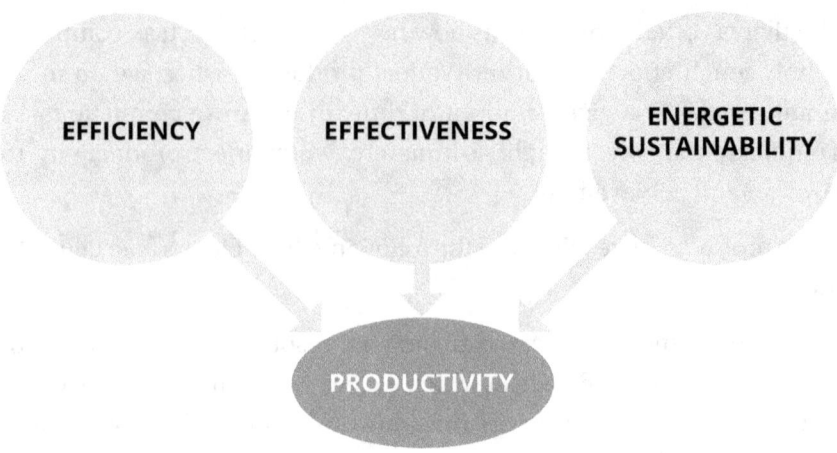

Figure 18: The three Es of productivity

The considerations listed in table 17 can help you become more efficient and effective and ensure energetic sustainability is high. These are applicable to individuals, but also teams and the wider workplace.

Table 17: Considerations for efficiency, effectiveness and energetic sustainability

Efficiency	<ul><li>Have I/we identified and minimised any unnecessary or time-consuming activities so I/we can work well?</li><li>Am I/are we delegating tasks appropriately or working in teams?</li><li>Do I/we have systems in place to streamline repetitive tasks or processes?</li><li>Have I/we set realistic deadlines and checkpoints to track progress, and are these visible?</li><li>Am I/are we leveraging available resources, such as tools, technology or support staff, to help with effectiveness?</li><li>Am I/are we prioritising tasks based on their importance and alignment with wider school objectives?</li></ul>

Effectiveness	• Do I/we understand the primary purpose or objective of this task? • Is it clear and understood how this task contributes to the overall goals or mission of the project, team or school? • Have I/we clearly defined the desired outcomes or success criteria for this task, and do I/we know/agree to what 'finished' looks like? • Is there a more efficient or impactful way to achieve the same goal? • Are there any alternative approaches or solutions that could enhance the task's impact? • Am I/are we regularly evaluating the results and impact of completed tasks to inform future decisions?
Energetic sustainability	• Am I/are we prioritising tasks based on their importance and the energy needed to complete the task? • Do I/we have a balance between tasks that energise me/us and those that may drain my/our energy? • Have I/we scheduled regular breaks throughout the day to recharge and establish any habits or routines that help to avoid ongoing stress and intense work periods, yet sustain energy levels throughout the day? • Are there opportunities to delegate tasks or collaborate with others to lighten workload for individuals and teams? • Am I/are we setting realistic expectations and allowing flexibility in the schedule to accommodate unexpected challenges? • Have I/we established boundaries to protect my/our energy and prevent overcommitment? • Do I/we regularly reflect on my/our energy levels and adjust the workload or priorities accordingly?

Workplace operations

Systems, structures and processes are closely tied to the often concealed or unknown methods of working in a school. In education, we're not always clear on what our operational procedures are. We don't often allocate time to thoroughly think them through or plan them, let alone making them visible or reviewing and changing them.

There is a difference between how a business works and how a school operates. In a business, standard operating procedures (SOPs) are common. SOPs are known and visible methods for how things are done, utilising efficient and effective processes that are consistent. They provide staff with clear steps to follow and exemplars of what a finished product looks like. They support productivity by reducing the number of decisions needing to be made about how to do tasks, and giving staff a clear example of what 'good enough' means.

We don't tend to have SOPs in education. We don't always know which steps to take, what the finished product should look like or when something is 'good enough'. This lack of clarity significantly contributes to reduced productivity and lowers workplace wellbeing.

Each school, system and state has different systems, processes and procedures for how things are done. Sometimes different teams within a school have different ways of working, too. Processes for things such as planning to assessing, bookmarking expectations and how reports are written, filling out leave forms, adding items to a calendar, marking the roll or booking a room or meeting space may be different across teams even in the same school.

I can appreciate that we may need different processes for various reasons – buildings are different, staff are different, software is different – but the lack of clarity and consistency also makes being an educator even more complicated. I often wonder: if we streamlined some of these things right across the country, from school to school, would this help to reduce the stress associated with the day-to-day tasks we must all complete?

I know there is a great need for autonomy and flexibility for each school setting, but one of the issues with having so many unclear and different procedures and processes is that it can take an incredibly long time to learn 'the way we do it around here'. Many processes are part of corporate knowledge and not recorded, which is unhelpful in a profession where staff are now so transient and moving jobs more often than ever before.

While the idea of streamlining things across the state or country may not be something we can impact right here, right now, I want to ask you this: what are the systems, processes and procedures within your school? Within your teams? How do staff work? Are these known? Are these visible? Are these easily understood by a new staff member? If not, there is some work to be done.

How planning is done, reports are written, assessments are organised and data is inputted should be the same from team to team across your school. The process for each task should be known by everyone, and be consistent and clear. Each task should come with easy-to-follow steps and guidelines in a central place everyone can access, and include clear examples of what finished looks like, not passed down like a secret family recipe, with bits missing and without a photo or example in sight.

Systems, structures and processes should be clear and visible. Without this, we are unknowingly inhibiting productivity, creating inconsistencies and misalignments among staff and teams, and adding more work to everyone's plates and increasing cognitive load. Not having well-thought-out or planned procedures or processes makes it difficult for staff to be effective, efficient and energetically sustainable.

Overall factors

Productivity is not only influenced by the three Es or the systems, structures and processes we have in place. There are many other factors that contribute to our level of productivity. For example, when we are tired or experiencing stress at home we can be distracted and easily disengaged; when we are unwell we find it hard to focus and work as effectively as we normally would. There are many factors that can impact productivity, all of which need to be considered to ensure we put the best support systems in place for individuals, teams and workplaces.

According to research institute RAND Europe (2015), the components that impact productivity fit into three categories:

1. Job and workplace-related factors, which include aspects of the work environment such as work demands, work relationships and corporate attitudes towards health and wellbeing.
2. Personal factors including personal attitudes to work and absence, and individual behaviour, such as lifestyle.
3. Mental and physical health factors, including existing (long-term) health conditions as well as things such as blood pressure and cholesterol levels.

As figure 19 shows, productivity is not the responsibility of the workplace alone, but includes a multitude of factors significant to the individual, all of which interlink and intertwine. Hence, when productivity is low or not as we would like it to be, we can't blame the task itself or what is happening solely in the workplace. We need to bring self-awareness, and awareness of what others may be experiencing, to appreciate the full picture of why productivity may be low. By doing this, we can look to allocate resources, find solutions and consider longer-term responses that may be needed. Low productivity should not be the norm, but we need to understand why it is in order to apply a useful strategy.

Figure 19: Overall factors for productivity
Adapted from RAND Europe, 2015.

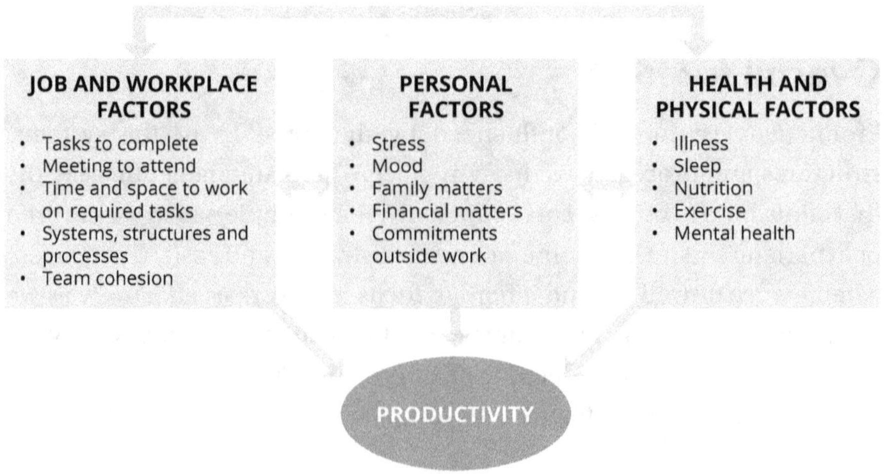

JOB AND WORKPLACE FACTORS
- Tasks to complete
- Meeting to attend
- Time and space to work on required tasks
- Systems, structures and processes
- Team cohesion

PERSONAL FACTORS
- Stress
- Mood
- Family matters
- Financial matters
- Commitments outside work

HEALTH AND PHYSICAL FACTORS
- Illness
- Sleep
- Nutrition
- Exercise
- Mental health

PRODUCTIVITY

The unhelpful productivity loop

Failure to incorporate the contributors to productivity can create in us a sense of going through the motions, where we are unable to achieve what we want while always adding more to our to-do list. When we're in this state we often find ourselves completing meaningless tasks that are considerably time-consuming, and that could be done more effectively if we reviewed and updated the systems, processes and structures in place.

Without making time and space to do this, we can unknowingly contribute to staff and teams feeling stuck, disengaged and like they are unable to do their job properly. This feeling of stagnation then works against how we are wanting to feel, causing us to procrastinate, become frustrated and slow down productivity, even though we are wanting to do the opposite. We can find ourselves in what I call the unhelpful productivity loop (see figure 20).

Figure 20: The unhelpful productivity loop

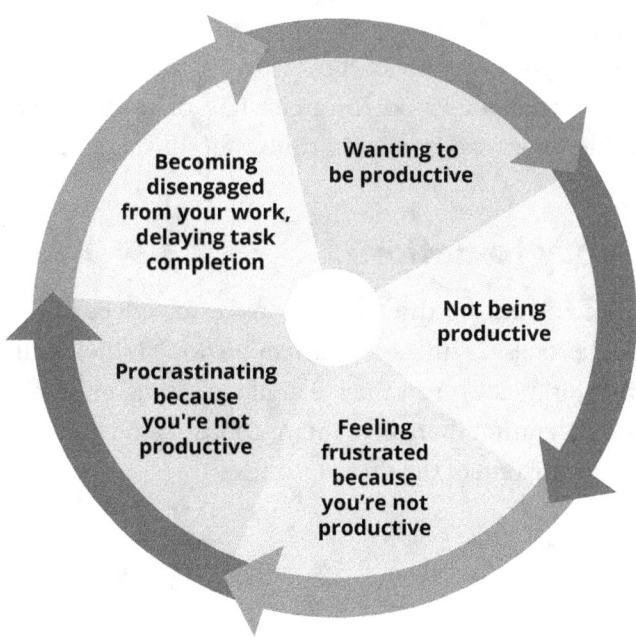

To move out of this unhelpful loop, we have to be open to new ways of doing things. We must refine how we work and hold ourselves accountable to incorporating the contributors to productivity into our working lives. While finding a new way to do a task can help with productivity, so too can stopping something. At times, we need to utilise the skills we have in teams, across the workplace, or individually to increase productivity by becoming more efficient, effective and ensuring we are working in a way that is energetically sustainable.

Chapter summary

- Contributors to productivity include the three Es of productivity, workplace operations and overall factors.
- The three Es of productivity include efficiency, effectiveness and energetic sustainability.
- Systems, structures and processes should be made visible, clear and consistent as much as possible.
- Life outside of work can impact productivity, including things such as sleep, nutrition and movement.
- We need to continually review how we are working individually, in teams and across our school through a lens of productivity to reap the benefit of improved wellbeing and staff satisfaction.

From theory to action

Choose a task and utilise the table opposite to reflect on the systems, structures and processes utilised (this can be done individually, in teams or across the workplace). You may also like to focus on a few questions from each section rather than all of them, choosing the most applicable to the task, or utilising one of the three Es only.

Task:	
Things to consider	**Answers**
Efficiency	
Have I/we identified and minimised any unnecessary or time-consuming activities so I/we can work well?	
Am I/are we delegating tasks appropriately or working in teams?	
Do I/we have systems in place to streamline repetitive tasks or processes?	
Have I/we set realistic deadlines and checkpoints to track progress, and are these visible?	
Am I/are we leveraging available resources, such as tools, technology or support staff, to help with effectiveness?	
Am I/are we prioritising tasks based on their importance and alignment with wider school objectives?	
Effectiveness	
Do I/we understand the primary purpose or objective of this task?	
Is it clear and understood how this task contributes to the overall goals or mission of the project, team or school?	
Have I/we clearly defined the desired outcomes or success criteria for this task, and do I/we know/agree to what 'finished' looks like?	
Is there a more efficient or impactful way to achieve the same goal?	
Are there any alternative approaches or solutions that could enhance the task's impact?	
Am I/are we regularly evaluating the results and impact of completed tasks to inform future decisions?	

Things to consider	Answers
Energetic sustainability Am I/are we prioritising tasks based on their importance and the energy needed to complete the task? Do I/we have a balance between tasks that energise me/us and those that may drain my/our energy? Have I/we scheduled regular breaks throughout the day to recharge and establish any habits or routines that help to avoid ongoing stress and intense work periods, yet sustain energy levels throughout the day? Are there opportunities to delegate tasks or collaborate with others to lighten workload for individuals and teams? Am I/are we setting realistic expectations and allowing flexibility in the schedule to accommodate unexpected challenges? Have I/we established boundaries to protect my/our energy and prevent overcommitment? Do I/we regularly reflect on my/our energy levels and adjust the workload or priorities accordingly?	

Application to a wellbeing-centred workplace

Feel well	Work well	Team well	Lead well
Productivity increases when we feel well, and we feel well when we are productive. To maximise this relationship, consider how you check in with your body and environment to increase productivity.	To work well, we need to ensure our processes and operations are known, visible and clear. Continually review these across all tasks to ensure you can work well.	As a team, utilise the language and approach of the three Es to continually reflect on efficiency, effectiveness and working in an energetically sustainable way.	As leaders we need to consider the overall factors for ourselves, our teams and across the workplace. This will ensure we are considering all aspects of productivity.

Chapter 11

Engagement

By enhancing work engagement we can create a positive workplace culture and increase staff wellbeing, including physical health, energy levels, job satisfaction and fulfilment. Engagement brings about benefits in many areas, so we need to seek out ways to ensure we are engaged at an individual and collective level.

The more engaged staff are at work, the more likely they are to attend, meaning they take fewer sick days and are more productive during the time they spend in the workplace. This has a direct impact on our ability to do our jobs as leaders, meaning we should actively aim to promote and increase staff engagement.

Like many other aspects of wellbeing, engagement varies in definition and behaviour from person to person. High engagement for one person may look different to another based on how people operate, externally and internally. Understanding that engagement varies can help us to create a diverse approach that extends beyond someone simply doing their job.

Engagement has been described as:

- 'Individuals' commitment to their work, their satisfaction from their work and the enthusiasm they feel about their work' (Robbins and Judge, 2012).
- 'A positive behavior or a state of mind that leads to positive results in the work. Work engagement is defined as effective and positive cognitive state, vigor, commitment, and absorption' (Roozeboom and Schelvis, 2015).
- 'When people express themselves physically, cognitively and mentally during work roles' (Kahn, 1990).

These definitions highlight a vast spectrum of meaning, which in some ways makes it difficult to know where to focus our time and energy, and how to make engagement meaningful for staff. To avoid getting bogged down, I suggest focusing on three key areas to promote engagement in a meaningful and practical way as part of creating a wellbeing-centred workplace: collaboration, team engagement and recognition.

Collaboration

In schools, collaboration is often reserved for when we come together to work on tasks to improve student learning. But there are so many other ways we could be collaborating in schools. Collaboration can boost individual and team engagement, and when this happens, further collaboration is more likely to occur. Collaboration and engagement go hand-in-hand.

When staff collaborate, they feel a sense of belonging, connection and support. Collaboration also ensures colleagues and teams are working together on shared outcomes, increasing knowledge and skills, and refining practice. Collaboration can also move educators from a top-down compliancy-based mindset to having a greater sense of social motivation (Kanold, 2011), which has many benefits for workplace wellbeing.

As well as collaborating to improve student learning, collaboration can also be a useful strategy to implement when we are reflecting on data and generating ideas to improve staff engagement, wellbeing and culture. By creating a collective approach and establishing a solutions-focused mindset among staff, coming together to problem-solve around areas such as workload, time pressures and stress factors can create a shared responsibility in a space where perhaps collaboration wasn't considered a strategy.

When considering opportunities to work collaboratively, we also need to distinguish between collaboration and working as a team. Collaboration is working together on the same goal, with the same vision, while teamwork is working individually towards the same goal. For example, planning individually and sharing these insights with colleagues is teamwork, whereas planning together, contributing, challenging ideas and adding to the same document at the same time is collaboration.

Collaboration is also extremely beneficial when working on challenging tasks. A study conducted by Stanford University showed collaboration caused participants to pursue tasks for 64 per cent longer than when working individually (Carr and Walton, 2014).

As with many other factors that contribute to workplace wellbeing, collaboration can't be left to chance. It needs to be intentionally designed, include clear guidelines and be used for a specific purpose (see table 18).

Table 18: Three things to consider when utilising collaboration

Purpose	What goal or outcome are we trying to achieve?	Before engaging in collaboration, the purpose needs to be very clear – including goals and how they will be met, factoring in checkpoints along the way. Failure to clarify the purpose increases the chance of more meetings, and no educator needs that.
Design	What are each person's roles and responsibilities?	Each person needs to be clear on the role they play and how they contribute, add value and actively participate. It is wise to consider people's strengths and how to use these when collaborating – otherwise, we risk some people doing all the work, and others not being included or opting out.
Guidelines	How do we engage and communicate with one another?	Collaboration requires communication and open, robust dialogue. We need to ensure guidelines are established for managing conflict and difficult conversations that may arise.

Team engagement

Engagement is not only amplified through meaningful and purposeful work, but also how staff work together. We can create a deeper sense of engagement in the workplace by fostering team engagement, ensuring it goes far beyond attending meetings together, focusing on surface-level tasks or supporting each other by covering lunch duty or collecting the photocopying.

Team engagement and overall engagement are connected, but are not the same. Staff engagement measures the commitment an individual feels towards their company and their willingness to go above and beyond to perform well, whereas team engagement looks at how staff interact with each other in a way that is most conducive to reaching company goals (Kelly, 2021).

To embed team engagement, we need collective responsibility, accountability and action (see figure 21). These three areas combined create the magic formula to true collective team support. When we take responsibility and action together and hold one another accountable, support becomes purposeful and meaningful, not just transactional.

Figure 21: Team engagement

Collective responsibility

Collective responsibility underpins collective support as it brings everyone together, so that no one is working in isolation. In teams, this looks like sharing responsibility for learning, student outcomes, planning, assessment, moderation, excursions, assemblies and so on. This understanding of collective responsibility strengthens engagement as individuals see and feel that they are part of a wider collective, with shared responsibility for all team tasks. Collective responsibility also removes the notion of blame, finding fault or team members stepping back from tasks. Similar to collaboration, it invites everyone into the space to strengthen engagement.

Collective accountability

Collective accountability builds a sense of clarity through creating more frequent, tangible checkpoints when working on specific tasks. Collective accountability means tasks are identified, agreed upon and reviewed together. Within collective accountability everyone is responsible for ensuring checkpoints are adhered to and followed through. Engagement is strengthened through this opportunity as teams work together on shared goals and tasks, supporting one another along the way.

Collective action

Collective action requires teams to move forward together. There is nothing worse than feeling like you are the only one working or moving forward while everyone else stands still or does their own thing. Collective action means everyone is doing the work at the same time, bringing together both collective accountability and responsibility. Without collective responsibility and accountability being established and set, action can start well and fade out, become ad-hoc, or take a different direction due to lack of team support.

When we think about boosting staff engagement, we cannot underestimate the power of how we build in team engagement through collective responsibility, accountability and action. We want staff to feel engaged not just with the work they do but with the people they work with. This will ultimately increase job satisfaction and the sense of belonging, both of which contribute to a culture of wellbeing.

Recognition

When we prioritise staff recognition, we are showing we value and appreciate the work our staff members do and the contribution they make, as well as enhancing their sense of accomplishment. This boosts engagement (Gallup, 2024).

Staff recognition can come in many forms: staff shout-outs, a note on a desk, a thank-you card or direct feedback. We need to recognise the work staff members do and the contribution that they make, helping them to see they are truly appreciated. In a school this can seem like a challenging task when there are so many things happening all the time and a lot of what is done is defined as 'part of the job'. This perception, though, can lead to staff completing tasks without recognition or celebration of how they are adding value to the workplace, as opposed to just getting things done. Recognition shouldn't be reserved for those who go above and beyond the expected job. When we do this we create a culture of overworking, and emphasise that the more we do, the more valued we are. We should acknowledge all the work staff do, which exists in all tasks, big and small, not only when someone goes 'above and beyond'.

According to Gallup (2024), the best managers promote a recognition-rich environment, encouraging praise from all directions, knowing people like to receive praise in different ways. It also recommends recognition be frequent (averaging once a week) and timely, and aligned with the workplace's purpose and culture to reflect its identity.

To ensure recognition is meaningful, I recommend making it:

- **Regular:** Positive feedback needs to occur often. Waiting until the end of term, the fortnightly meeting where one person is singled out, or relying on ad-hoc, random staff shout-outs does not fulfil what is required for staff to feel recognised and valued in the workplace. We provide regular, timely and specific feedback to students, and we need to do the same for staff.
- **Personalised:** Not everyone likes to be recognised in the same way, at the same time, in the same mode each time. Recognition should be personalised. Some people like public recognition and some don't; some like a written note and others a kind word; some like a

chocolate on their desk and others a pat on the back. It is important to know how each person likes to be recognised so recognition can be specific and meaningful – otherwise, recognition may not have the desired impact. The best way to find out how staff members like to be recognised is to ask them. You could do this via a survey at the start of the year, asking staff to select options from a list to indicate how they like to receive recognition. This information can also be shared among staff so colleagues know how to best show each other they are valued.
- **Values-aligned:** Providing recognition should align with the collective values of the workplace or team. This highlights the contribution staff are making to the wider vision and upholds the core values of the team and workplace.

Along with this, it's also valuable to recognise staff members' personal achievements and celebrations – for example, competing in a sporting event, having a baby, completing study or engaging in charity work. This not only increases engagement but provides a sense of belonging and ensures staff members are seen not just for the work they do but the person they are.

Chapter summary

- Increased engagement can positively impact staff wellbeing, including physical health, energy levels, job satisfaction and positive workplace culture.
- In a school setting, we should look to increase collaboration through building team engagement and recognition.
- Collaboration can't be left to chance – it needs to be intentionally designed, including clear guidelines, and used for a specific purpose.
- Team engagement refers to how staff interact with each other in a way that is most in line with reaching school goals, and is achieved through collective responsibility, accountability and action.
- To ensure recognition is meaningful, it needs to be regular, personalised and in line with workplace or team values.

From theory to action

Consider the three areas needed to increase staff engagement: collaboration, team engagement and recognition. Reflect on your current state and goal, and note down three actions you could take towards your goals.

	Current state	Goal	Actions to take
Collaboration			
Team engagement			
Recognition			

Application to a wellbeing-centred workplace

Feel well	Work well	Team well	Lead well
By boosting engagement, we are also positively impacting our physical, mental and emotional wellbeing. Engagement can make us feel happier and more energised, and increase our sense of enjoyment at work, rippling into other areas of life.	Increased engagement supports us to work well. The more engaged we are, the more productive we may be and the more motivated we feel, benefiting overall satisfaction at work.	Engagement links closely to how we team. Increasing team engagement allows us to function more effectively as a cohesive unit.	Within leadership, staff recognition is paramount to increasing engagement. If we are able to do this in a timely, meaningful and personalised way, we are showing staff they are valued and appreciated as well as reinforcing workplace values.

Chapter 12

Performance and Growth

A growth mindset, continuous improvement, feedback cycles, PD – all of these contribute to a culture that values performance and growth, yet they are often not as openly embraced as we may like. In an already overwhelming working environment, how do we bring about a culture of growth and a standard of high performance when it seems like another thing to add to the list?

First, we need to understand that change, growth and evolution are part of not just the workplace, but life. It's an inevitable phase that exists and we need to recognise when it is desired, required or unavoidable.

The need to ensure performance and growth exists in all Australian schools is reinforced by the Australian Institute for Teaching and School Leadership (AITSL) Australian Teacher Performance and Development Framework (AITSL, 2012). This framework suggests all schools should have a performance and development culture, so educators know what is expected of them, receive frequent and meaningful feedback, and receive high-quality support to improve practice.

However, the challenge with growth and performance is that it can feel overwhelming, like an extra task that diverts focus from our current work. This can lead to what is sometimes referred to as 'growth fatigue' or 'growth resistance', where any push for improvement is met with frustration, resistance and discomfort.

It's easy to understand why this mindset exists in a school environment, where educators are already stretched thin, changes occur frequently and we often move from one initiative to the next without fully embedding the first. Most growth in schools is about continuous change, not continuous improvement as it should be. To support educators to be open to continued growth and performance, we need to find the balance between introducing new initiatives and pausing to embed and integrate our current priorities.

As a leader in a wellbeing-centred school, reflecting on this balance is crucial. Linking growth and performance initiatives to current priorities can help to avoid the perception that growth is merely an add-on or an increase in workload for no meaningful reason.

Ultimately, we need to value the idea of performing to a high standard and the growth we need to undertake to do so. This requires us to implement many things that, in Australian schools, can be perceived as a little taboo or like the elephant in the room: feedback cycles, PD, peer reviews and performance reviews. Yes, it must be said that in education in Australia we don't always do these things well. Again, it is an area that is different from school to school, system to system, but one that needs to be addressed.

There are three areas I recommend focusing on to embed a culture of performance and growth:

- Professional development (PD)
- Feedback
- Accountability.

Professional development

Professional development (PD) is a key area all educators must engage in to improve practice and performance. There is a multitude of conferences, online courses, events, workshops and webinars available to us year after year. However, PD can also occur in informal contexts such as discussions among work colleagues, independent reading and research, observations of a colleague's work, or other learning from a peer (Mizel, 2010).

PD is an opportunity for people to learn and grow in an area that supports their practice, allowing them to learn new strategies for situations that may be challenging. According to the State Government of Victoria (n.d.), when a school culture is one of 'collaborative professionalism', teachers become investigators of their own practice and work together to find evidence-based solutions to problems of practice. Therefore, the more we build a culture of ongoing PD, utilising this in whole school, team and individual opportunities, the more we are able to work together to seek solutions and create better learning environments for students. This not only builds our capacity as educators, but enhances our wellbeing through elevating an internal need to grow. When this is done well it can also increase areas of psychological wellbeing such as meaning fulfilment and purpose, as we know what we're doing in our workday is valuable, needed and impactful.

Feedback

Feedback is essential to performance and growth. As educators and leaders we need to be open to seeking and providing feedback in multiple ways, regularly, to improve practice. Within our classroom we often provide students with feedback in order to move their learning forward. Just as it helps them to know where they are going and where to next, what is working well and what can be improved, or what to focus on to move to the next level, we, as educators and leaders, benefit in the same way.

Feedback supports building a culture of wellbeing, as the more comfortable we become with giving and receiving feedback, the more likely we are to ask for support and help. It can also give people skills to address conflict before it escalates (Miles, 2022). Feedback should be part of regular practice, not dependent on role title, position or hierarchy. It should be available to everyone from everyone, and built into culture.

While there are many ways to give and receive feedback, to build a culture of wellbeing we want to ensure feedback is open, honest, and delivered in a way that allows staff to feel safe and supported. One key way to do this is to utilise peer evaluations.

Peer evaluations are a great way to build connections between staff members, increase engagement, and provide a safe and supportive way for colleagues to engage and grow together. Receiving feedback from peers helps staff understand their performance and creates a strong culture of frequent feedback in the team (Stone, 2023).

When conducting peer evaluations, we are inviting people to critique, reflect on and evaluate a colleague's performance in an area that is best identified as a team goal, where all members are being reviewed in the same area, or an area identified by the person being reviewed.

While there are many ways peer evaluations can be conducted, there are some essential steps to follow, which I have outlined in table 19.

Along with peer evaluations, feedback also needs to come from leadership. The same process for peer review can be applied here. What is most important to note is that the purpose, intention and desired impact of providing feedback is understood by all involved.

At times, receiving feedback from leaders – be it informal, within a meeting about something that has occurred, or after a lesson observation – is not always seen in the best light. This can be due to fear that feedback from a leader is for performance management rather than part of a process of continuous growth and improvement. We must acknowledge that it is a leader's responsibility to monitor, review and reflect on the performance of staff so areas of growth can be identified and continuous improvement ensured. In no way should a leader enter this space to identify what's wrong, to make someone feel inadequate, or to increase stress or pressure. Feedback in any workplace is essential for performance and growth, even if it's uncomfortable at times, but it must be delivered clearly, objectively and kindly.

The impact of feedback delivered well is twofold. First, it fosters a positive relationship between a leader and their staff, increasing trust and openness between them. Second, it ensures educators know where to focus on to perform well and grow. When it's delivered clearly and kindly, feedback can reduce ambiguity – following feedback, an educator will know whether they are doing a good job, which areas they should prioritise in their efforts and whether or not they can feel satisfied and accomplished in the work they're doing. Without kind, clear and specific feedback from leaders, many educators are left wondering whether what they're doing is right, enough, or at the standard their workplace expects. When this occurs, uncertainty and lack of job clarity can be evident, which negatively impacts workplace wellbeing.

Self-awareness is paramount to the feedback process, for the giver and receiver. So too is ensuring a psychologically safe workplace is established, which we will explore in the next chapter.

Table 19: Essential steps to a peer review

What this means	Why this matters
Step 1: Decide who is observing whom	
Identify whether one person or a group will observe another and if this will be reciprocated or shared around. It is common for person A to observe person B and then swap, but this doesn't always have to be the case.	We want staff to feel comfortable in this process to ensure they are confident and succeed. That said, we also need to become open to receiving feedback from multiple people and, over time, this may mean engaging in a peer review with a colleague who is outside a staff member's immediate team, as well as leadership.
Step 2: Set an individual or shared goal	
A goal is essential so the person being observed knows what to focus on, and so the observer knows what to look for. Keep the goal narrow and make it clear. Decide if this will be the same for everyone or different.	Observations and giving feedback can be challenging. The more specific and narrow our goal, the more we can ensure we are supporting staff to feel a sense of achievement as well as knowing where to focus their time and energy when preparing.
Step 3: Be clear on what to look for and what the standard of excellence is	
Once a goal is established, create some outcomes that will be used as success markers during the review process. Just as we utilise a rubric with students, work examples and modelling, we can apply the same here, ensuring all staff have the opportunity to achieve success.	This is often an overlooked step and one that is required. Without this we do not know what the standard for success is. This creates uncertainty and ambiguity, which can impact wellbeing.

What this means	Why this matters
Step 4: Decide on what else (if anything) may need to be shared	
What else may need to be shared for a successful peer review process? For example, the observer may require lesson plans in advance, or an understanding of class dynamics and student groupings, or to see the resources. This is all optional but something to consider.	More information may be needed to ensure the full picture is understood and so the person being observed feels they have done all they can to demonstrate their competence. We need to give staff this opportunity to shine. Creating multiple scaffolds for success increases motivation, a key driver of wellbeing.
Step 5: Conduct reviews and reflect	
Make a time for the review. Ensure there is plenty of notice, and space/time to do this – including time to record notes and prepare these for feedback. Note-taking allows for all ideas to be caught as they are in front of mind.	We need to be open and embrace this space. This is how we create a high sense of performance and growth in our schools, and with each other.
Step 6: Give feedback	
Allow the observer to provide feedback based on their own reflection before offering feedback yourself. Often the observer will have identified their own areas for growth, with which you can agree, elaborate or add to. When giving feedback, align it to the goal set at the beginning of the process.	Feedback builds a culture of wellbeing by creating open and honest dialogue between colleagues. This is known to increase engagement and connection, and enhance how staff work together.
Step 7: Identify next steps	
Identify two things that can be implemented following the feedback that both the observer and the person being observed agree are the most useful at this time.	Without next steps the purpose for peer evaluation and feedback becomes obsolete. Ideally, these steps are continually referred to, becoming part of the continuous improvement cycle.

Accountability

'Accountability' – perhaps the most taboo word in this whole book.

Let's be clear: having high levels of accountability does not mean as a leader you lack trust in your staff, you're micromanaging them or you're trying to be on top of every little thing they are doing.

Accountability through a wellbeing-leadership lens helps to remove the unknown, the unclear and the question 'Is this enough?' It's essential that we create expectations that are clear so staff know what is expected of them, and that we can easily and accurately answer the question 'Is this enough?' Accountability is more than just checking if someone is doing their job. It is about providing clear guidelines and expectations, and supporting people to efficiently and effectively meet these so they can do their job confidently, well and with autonomy.

When done well, accountability can help to improve staff mental health, increase productivity, and enhance growth and performance. Darren Finkelstein (2023), author of *The Accountability Advantage*, says accountability means honouring commitments, being reliable, and owning successes and failures. Brené Brown (2018) identifies accountability as one of the seven pillars of trust, stating accountability means you own your mistakes, apologise and make amends. Accountability also links to self-awareness as it requires a high level of self-responsibility.

To truly understand accountability as a means to build a wellbeing-centred workplace, we need to know what it is and what it isn't. I've outlined this in table 20 (overleaf).

Accountability is not only crucial to performance and growth in the workplace, but also to how teams function. And, as we have learned, the teams we work in and how teams in our workplace operate contribute significantly to building a wellbeing-centred workplace. Lencioni (2002) states that avoiding accountability may be one of the five reasons teams are dysfunctional. According to Lencioni, there are five behaviours to build to ensure accountability is developed: trust, managing conflict, committing to decisions, team accountability, and focusing on achieving collective results.

We can see from these five behaviours that accountability is a multilayered mechanism that is more than just ensuring people meet deadlines.

It requires trust, difficult conversations and knowing how to approach uncomfortable topics with one another, deciding on what needs to be done and committing to agreed expectations, utilising team accountability and achieving collective results.

What's important is that we approach accountability in a way that promotes a sense of connectedness and engagement, and through a lens of performance and growth. Accountability is up to everyone, not just a leader or manager.

Table 20: Accountability in a wellbeing-centred workplace

What it is	What it isn't
• **Taking responsibility:** Owning your tasks and decisions, and their outcomes. • **Transparency:** Being open and honest about progress, challenges and mistakes. • **Commitment:** Following through on commitments and promises. • **Feedback acceptance:** Being receptive to constructive criticism and using it to improve. • **Proactiveness:** Anticipating problems and addressing them before they escalate. • **Reliability:** Consistently meeting deadlines and delivering quality work. • **Communication:** Keeping team members informed and engaged about progress and any issues. • **Continuous improvement:** Seeking ways to improve performance and processes. • **Collaboration:** Working effectively with others to achieve common goals. • **Ethical behaviour:** Upholding integrity and ethical standards in all actions.	• **Blame-shifting:** Deflecting responsibility onto others when things go wrong. • **Micromanaging:** Over-controlling or dictating every detail of how tasks should be done. • **Avoiding consequences:** Dodging the repercussions of your actions or decisions. • **Excuses:** Justifying poor performance instead of addressing the root causes. • **Indifference:** Showing a lack of concern for the quality or outcome of work. • **Withholding information:** Failing to share important updates or issues with the team. • **Inconsistency:** Being unreliable or unpredictable in meeting commitments. • **Passivity:** Waiting for problems to be brought up instead of actively identifying and solving them. • **Isolated work:** Not engaging with team members or avoiding collaboration. • **Unethical practices:** Compromising on integrity and ethics for short-term gains.

Chapter summary

- Change, growth and evolution are part of not just the workplace, but life.
- A growth mindset, continuous improvement, feedback cycles and PD all contribute to a culture of performance and growth.
- There are three areas to focus on when creating a wellbeing-centred culture through performance and growth: PD, feedback and accountability.
- Creating a culture of feedback can increase productivity and engagement, and also people's ability to ask for help before reaching crisis point, providing an opportunity to intervene early and improve wellbeing quickly.
- Accountability means owning mistakes, following through on commitments, cultivating trust and knowing how to manage conflict.

From theory to action

With accountability being a key contributor to how staff work, I've listed some reflection questions below that I encourage you to use to begin a conversation with your staff.

Professional development

- How do you currently engage in PD within our workplace?
- Can you share examples of formal and informal PD activities you've participated in recently?
- In your opinion, what role does PD play in improving practice and performance in our school?
- How do you think we can ensure consistency and clarity in our approach to PD?
- What are your thoughts on the idea of 'collaborative professionalism' as described in the text, and how do you see it being implemented in our workplace?

Feedback

- How do you currently perceive feedback within our workplace, and how does it contribute to your professional growth?
- Can you share any experiences you've had with giving and receiving feedback, either through formal channels or informal interactions?
- In your opinion, what role does peer review play in fostering a culture of wellbeing and continuous improvement among colleagues?
- How do you think we can ensure that feedback, both from peers and leadership, is constructive, open and supportive?
- What steps do you believe are essential in conducting effective peer reviews, and how can we implement these practices in our workplace?

Accountability

- How do you perceive the role of accountability in our workplace, particularly in relation to PD and growth?
- Can you share any experiences you've had with accountability and how it has impacted your PD?
- In your opinion, how does accountability contribute to fostering a culture of wellbeing?
- What steps or strategies do you think we can implement to ensure accountability is approached in a way that promotes connection, engagement and growth among team members?
- How do you believe accountability aligns with the broader goals of PD and enhancing team effectiveness, as discussed in the text?

Application to a wellbeing-centred workplace

Feel well	Work well	Team well	Lead well
When we know we are performing well and growing, our sense of self enhances. This positively impacts our mental and emotional health and increases positive emotions.	By embracing PD, feedback and accountability in all areas of work, we are focusing on working well.	Without accountability we risk operating in dysfunctional teams. To team well, PD, feedback and accountability are essential. Peer evaluations also strengthen our ability to team well.	As leaders, we need to put structures in place to ensure PD, feedback and accountability are done well. We don't rush or overlook these things, but instead value and understand the need for this so we can lead well.

Chapter 13

Psychological Safety

Creating a psychologically safe working environment is key to workplace wellbeing. In many ways I have saved the most important topic in this book for last.

Creating a safe workplace has perhaps become just as common in the education vernacular as words such as 'wellbeing' and 'resilience'. Yet like many of the areas we know need improving, unless we develop a shared understanding, and ensure collective responsibility and action takes place, nothing will change or improve.

For some time now, we have thought of a safe workplace in terms of physical safety, under the banner of occupational health and safety. Yet to build a wellbeing-centred workplace, we need to focus on psychological safety *and* consider psychosocial risk. We cannot expect any of the previously mentioned characteristics to be present if we don't ensure psychological safety. Wellbeing improves when psychological safety is high.

As the terms 'psychological safety' and 'psychosocial hazards' are often used together, let's take a look at some definitions to understand the distinction (see table 21 overleaf).

Table 21: Key definitions
Adapted from Safety Australia, 2023.

Psychological safety	Psychological safety occurs in a work environment in which staff feel safe to express themselves and take risks without fear of negative consequences such as humiliation, punishment or discrimination. Psychological safety is a positive attribute, as it fosters an environment in which staff feel valued, respected and able to speak up.
Psychosocial risks	Psychosocial risks refer to work-related factors that may have negative effects on a person's mental health and wellbeing due to job demands such as excessive workloads, time pressure, low job control, role ambiguity or conflict. Psychosocial risks may also include issues related to work-life balance, such as long work hours, job insecurity, and inadequate support for work-life balance.

Figure 22 shows examples of psychosocial risks and barriers to psychological safety, and how these overlap.

Figure 22: Psychosocial risks and barriers to psychological safety
Adapted from MiTraining, n.d.

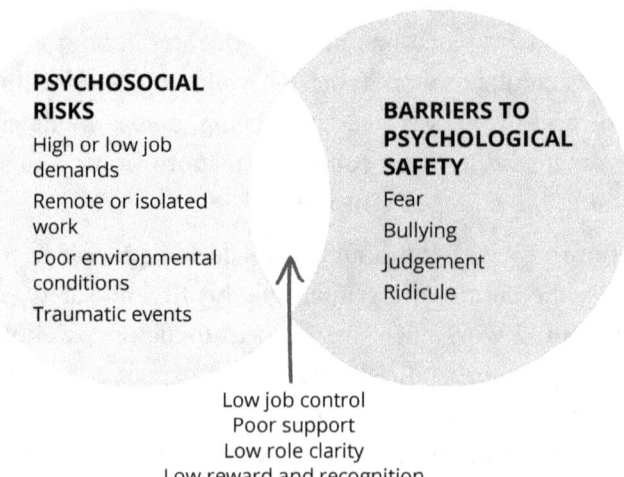

Many of these factors can coexist or influence other risks and barriers to be present. For example, remote or isolated work may lead to poor support, and poor organisational change management could impact workplace relationships.

Identifying these risks and barriers is helpful, but we must also consider how to actively shift and address them. With each school being unique with its own context, nuances and circumstances, creating a psychologically safe workplace with low psychosocial risk is not as simple as we may like it to be.

No two schools, whether within the same system or the same state, are alike. This is a wonderful aspect of schools, but it can also pose challenges. When we create singular strategies for multiple workplaces, such as schools, it can be difficult for each school to implement them effectively. Schools have varying numbers of pupils, resulting in different timetables, class sizes, subjects taught, planning processes, assessment cycles, marking processes, leadership structures, staff meeting schedules, strategic plans and PD opportunities. Additionally, the ways in which teams connect and collaborate differ. Essentially, every aspect of how a school functions, including its people, varies from one school to another, even those located nearby.

This means, as leaders, we must be willing to examine the individual components of our workplace with a microscope. We need to ask questions and analyse these factors with greater scrutiny than ever before, because how we integrate these diverse elements impacts the safety of our staff.

To truly comprehend what is transpiring in our workplace, it is insufficient to rely on assumptions, guesswork or presumed knowledge. We must be more open to collecting contextualised data that reflects our specific setting. This can be achieved through surveys, questionnaires, weekly check-ins or observation. However, the most effective method of capturing the essence of what is transpiring in your school is by engaging in dialogue with your staff – by asking questions and eliciting qualitative data, tailored to the specifics of your school. You can do this by creating what I refer to as a culture of speak and seek.

A culture of speak and seek

A culture high in psychological safety and that addresses psychosocial risks is one where speak and seek is evident. Speak and seek is a concept that ensures all staff members, whether they're in leadership roles, teaching positions or working in the canteen, actively engage in questioning and enquiring into the strengths, challenges and areas for improvement within the workplace.

Identifying areas for improvement does not solely rest with the leadership team; it requires collective responsibility, with everyone coming together. In a research paper exploring how to build psychological safety for teachers, Shahid and Din (2021) stated:

> *Leadership traits, orientations, and behavior may be the most important factors in shaping organizational culture, yet leaders cannot do it all by themselves. Each member of the organization and each team has to contribute to the culture, which would eventually improve the work environment for the employees.*

Failure to speak up about what might be causing stress and frustration or identify things that aren't working well denies leaders and colleagues the opportunity to step in, offer support, make changes or explore new and different ways of doing things. Similarly, failure to seek out the underlying causes of stress, frustration or things that aren't working can lead to assumptions without evidence, resulting in changes being implemented based on guesswork. Through speak and seek, we can become granular and specific about what is occurring, enabling us to address the root cause rather than just treating symptoms.

To do this well we need to go beyond words such as 'stressed', 'overwhelmed' or 'tired'. While these words may reflect how we are feeling, they do not provide us with insights or guidance on what to do next. It is important to acknowledge these feelings, but without identifying the reasons behind them, meaningful change cannot occur. Speak and seek allows us to ask questions, probe more deeply into ambiguous words, and work towards real strategic change.

To facilitate this, we must be comfortable sharing how we feel, discussing what impacts our wellbeing and workload, and what causes stress, while actively sharing new ideas and suggestions. We need to seek out this information by asking questions, listening, and ensuring we respond without judgement, criticism, defensiveness or dismissiveness.

However, it's important to note that even if staff feel comfortable speaking up and seeking out, consideration must still be given to whether their ideas are actioned or not. Some staff may express that they don't feel heard or valued if their ideas are not implemented. While an idea or suggestion not being implemented should not necessarily detract from someone feeling heard or valued, a lack of feedback or recurrent instances of ideas being disregarded without explanation can lead to disengagement and reluctance to speak up in the future.

We must also consider our own mental and emotional state before offering ideas and thoughts. Speaking up in a supportive, constructive manner, with compassion and grace, differs greatly from speaking up when our emotions are heightened, our thoughts unclear, or when we are not ready to engage in an open conversation about our concerns. It's crucial to approach conversations in a manner that maintains psychological safety for all parties involved.

A leader's role in creating psychological safety

As workplaces consider possibilities such as distributive leadership, breaking down old hierarchical models and encouraging staff voice and autonomy, staff often express that they also want to experience a safe working environment. However, creating this is not automatic. Doing so requires consideration for how staff feel, whether or not they are confident and comfortable to speak up, sharing challenges, concerns or new ideas, and doing so without feeling like they may be judged, shamed or critiqued, even if what they are saying goes against usual and existing ways of thinking.

Amy Edmondson defines psychological safety as 'the belief that one will not be punished or humiliated for speaking up with ideas, questions, concerns, or mistakes and that the team is safe for interpersonal risk-taking' (Edmondson, n.d.). Edmondson's research has shown that psychological safety can actually predict both group learning and group performance

(Learner Lab, n.d.). With this in mind, we must become aware of how, as leaders, we are contributing to the creation of psychological safety.

Ensuring all staff feel safe to speak up, share and question is not something that should be overlooked or left to chance – especially as this is a key component to ensuring we address staff wellbeing and culture through real and specific actions within schools.

As each school operates differently, the only way, at this point in time, to address things that impact staff wellbeing is to ensure we are speaking up and seeking out issues or ideas that are relevant to our school context. While it is also important to look at and address systemic issues in teaching, there is a significant amount we can do now if we are open, willing and ready to speak up about what is going on and to seek out concerns and new ideas.

As we move to having staff wellbeing at the centre of decision-making and the driver to improve school culture, taking time to consider how psychological safety is established, and addressing psychosocial health while including everyone in the process, is a crucial step.

Chapter summary

- Without creating a safe working environment, the other characteristics of a wellbeing-centred workplace may not be present.
- A safe workplace comprises psychological safety and reduced psychosocial risks.
- Psychological safety is present in a work environment in which staff feel safe to express themselves and take risks without fear of negative consequences.
- Psychosocial risks refer to work-related factors that may have negative effects on a person's mental health and wellbeing due to job demands such as excessive workloads, time pressure, low job control, role ambiguity or conflict.
- Creating a culture where speak and seek is embedded is the best way to discover the nuanced and context-specific ways to improve your workplace.

From theory to action

The table below includes suggested action points to embed the key ideas of this chapter into your school.

Psychological safety	Collect feedback from staff to identify where you need to focus in this area. This could be done via a survey or questionnaire, or through discussion groups. Include questions that gauge staff members' perceptions of their ability to speak up, share ideas, ask questions and take risks without fear of negative consequences. Also include questions about their level of trust in leadership and colleagues.
Psychosocial risks	It is imperative everyone becomes familiar with this topic. To do so please refer to Safe Work Australia: https://www.safeworkaustralia.gov.au/safety-topic/managing-health-and-safety/mental-health/psychosocial-hazards
Speak and seek	Consider how to build this into your workplace. This could include making time in meetings for a wellbeing check-in, hosting wellbeing speak and seek sessions each term, or offering drop-in sessions throughout the term to talk about certain topics. To support those hosting these sessions, ensure they have training and skills in coaching questions.

Application to a wellbeing-centred workplace

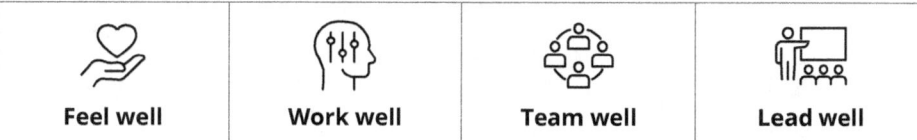

Feel well	Work well	Team well	Lead well

A safe workplace encompasses every one of these areas individually and collectively. Without addressing psychological safety, staff simply will not feel well, work well, team well or lead well.

It doesn't matter how much an individual prioritises or works on their own wellbeing and boosts their personal wellbeing strategies. If their workplace is not psychologically safe, there is only so much an individual can withstand. This is why it's essential to prioritise psychological safety and reduce psychosocial risks.

Conclusion

Where to Now?

While we are doing great things in schools, we can do many things better and some things differently. In the space of wellbeing leadership, it is not just about putting on morning teas and cancelling meetings to improve staff wellbeing; it's about how we work, who we are, what we do, who and how our staff are, how we feel, how we work in teams, and how we connect. It's about culture. It's also about workload, priorities and strategic plans, initiatives and pedagogical approaches, stress factors, deadlines and competing priorities; this too is culture, and as leaders, this is where the majority of our work should lie.

We need to focus on what matters. We need to make data-informed decisions and consider what changes we can make that will give us the biggest return on investment for staff wellbeing in the short and long term. This means not always doing the easiest, most appealing or fun thing. Instead, we need to embrace the true work of wellbeing. We have to be better at saying no, choosing some things for now and saving some for later, and not doing something even though we may want to. We have to recognise what we can control and do what we can with the capacity, energy and resources we have, rather than always adding more to our plate. This includes not just our core business of teaching and supporting students, but everything else in between.

I see a lot of schools fail to create impact in staff wellbeing because they don't make it a high enough priority. Wellbeing is muddled in with other priorities and activities, it's not planned well enough or it's an afterthought. We can't continue to do this. We can't let staff wellbeing become something that begins well but is forgotten. We can't leave it to a group of staff who don't really have the ability to influence change, so they default to morning teas. We can't squeeze wellbeing randomly into staff meetings because someone says, 'I thought we were focusing on staff wellbeing this year; we haven't done anything for a while.' This isn't good enough. It's not what will create the shift we need and it's not going to be how we turn our schools into thriving workplaces.

Moving forward, we need to ensure that everyone – educators, leaders and all school staff – understands what it means to address and improve staff wellbeing. We need to challenge what we think it is, and be really specific about what it actually is. This means intentionally designing our schools to be workplaces that value, prioritise and nurture staff wellbeing, that make time to address workload issues and stress factors, and that encourage new, creative solutions. To do this, there is one final piece left to consider: how to identify limitations, ask better questions and ideate sustainable and creative solutions.

Limitations, questions, solutions

I hope by this point in the book you are pondering ideas and possibilities, and feel hopeful about change. This is a great space to be in. It is here that we dream and allow ourselves to be creative, and that new ways of working can come to fruition. However, as I am sure you have experienced, when we share or express an idea, no matter how big or small, we are often met with limitations, barriers or excuses, either our own or from those around us. While this is common, it is also a key part of the change process. By identifying limitations and asking better questions, we can truly step into a space of creating the wellbeing-centred workplace all educators and staff deserve.

When looking to create change, make shifts or improve, limitations will become apparent; this is normal. We are wired to look for danger, and a limitation is what our brain sees as danger. However, once we start to understand that many limitations exist because of our own thinking, we can start to ask better questions, think outside the box and dream up new ideas.

In all the work I have done in schools over the past few years, despite coming up against many limitations, this process has led to significant change in a number of workplaces.

Table 22 demonstrates how we can take limitations or challenges and use key questions to dream up sustainable solutions.

Table 22: Limitations, questions, solutions

Identify limitations *(These are things that impact staff wellbeing.)*	**Ask better questions** *(These are questions to find out more information and identify cause and effect.)*	**Dream up solutions** *(These are ideas from staff.)*
'There is no structured or set time for team planning.'	When do you plan? What does this look like? How would a set time with structure help? What would be an appropriate amount of time? How could this be organised or structured? What would you like to achieve in these planning sessions? What would you like to focus on? What would you not like to focus on? What support do you need?	Timetable weekly or fortnightly planning sessions for teams. Organise team-planning days each term. Build planning time into staff PD days. Create scope and sequences for all subjects. Allocate staff member to planning or resourcing (based on strengths). Ensure leadership support is provided to guide planning sessions. Cycle planning and reviewing so new units are not being planned all of the time. Get ahead with planning cycles so it isn't happening at the same time as teaching.

Identify limitations *(These are things that impact staff wellbeing.)*	Ask better questions *(These are questions to find out more information and identify cause and effect.)*	Dream up solutions *(These are ideas from staff.)*
'We have too many last-minute interruptions.'	Can you give me some examples of this? What does this impact? Is there a time frame for what 'last minute' is? For example, the day before, the week before? When is last-minute okay? (Because sometimes it can't be avoided.) When is last-minute not okay? (Because sometimes it just shouldn't happen.) When something is last-minute, how does this impact how you feel and work? What ideas do you have to prevent last-minute interruptions from occurring?	Ensure the term calendar is complete and set before each term break (ideally, week 9 of each term). No new items to be added two weeks out. Additional weekly calendars to be sent on a Thursday before the following week (not on a Friday or Sunday). Last-minute changes require a face-to-face conversation or phone call. An email isn't reliable. If someone wants to add in a change outside the two-week window, be prepared to say and hear no. With staff, devise what is acceptable as a 'last-minute' interruption.

Identify limitations *(These are things that impact staff wellbeing.)*	Ask better questions *(These are questions to find out more information and identify cause and effect.)*	Dream up solutions *(These are ideas from staff.)*
'The vision is unclear; there are too many competing priorities.'	What is the current vision? Does everyone agree with this? What are the current priorities? Is everyone aware of these? How does each one impact how you feel and work? What do you think is a priority worth keeping? What priority do you think can be let go of or paused? How could priorities be implemented to support staff wellbeing?	Audit current visions and priorities. Review these and ask 'Are these still necessary?' and 'Do they align with our vision?' Consider pausing or letting go of some of these. Audit how much each priority asks of staff (in my work it has become apparent if every leader has a priority and they are asking something of staff, this can easily and quickly add up). Review through the lens of 'Do staff have the capacity for this?' Have a visual timeline of all priorities to see what is really being asked of staff. Consider a seasonal timeline for implementation – not all priorities need to start at the beginning of the year.

These examples are from no school in particular, however, they are real examples, some of which I have heard many times. When I run my Beneath the Surface days to capture qualitative data and to explore what is going on beyond various staff wellbeing surveys or words such as 'stressed' or 'overwhelmed', this is how specific we get. The more specific we are, the more we are able to change.

This is what can come out of wellbeing-centred decision-making, wellbeing leadership, a culture of speak and seek, and by identifying stressors and areas to improve. This, along with the eight characteristics of a wellbeing-centred workplace, will help you to undertake the transformation needed in your school.

A final message

Teaching is a great profession. We are its best advertisers, advocates and allies. We need to remain hopeful. We need to realise the power and autonomy we have. We need to be confident in the decisions we make and stand strong in them. We need to say no where we can, de-implement and do less. We need to set boundaries for ourselves and how our staff work. We need to be brave, bold and courageous. Most importantly, we need to recognise which areas in our schools we create, design and influence, because these are the areas we can also change, and these are the areas we can leverage now to create a wellbeing-centred workplace where staff want to work, educators want to teach, and people want to be.

It's over to you now: to lead with staff wellbeing in mind, to take risks, to embrace vuja de and think differently, and to be the leader you know you are.

References

AITSL. (2012). *Australian Teacher Performance and Development Framework.* https://www.aitsl.edu.au/tools-resources/resource/australian-teacher-performance-and-development-framework

American Psychological Association. (2020). *Building your resilience.* https://www.apa.org/topics/resilience/building-your-resilience

Bidilică, M. (2024.) *2023 Publishing Trends to Help Your Book Marketing This Year.* Publishdrive. https://publishdrive.com/book-publishing-trends.html

Bolte Taylor, J. (2009). *My Stroke of Insight.* Hodder & Stoughton.

Brown, B. (2018). *Dare to Lead.* Random House.

Cameron, K. et al. (2011). Effects of Positive Practices on Organizational Effectiveness. *The Journal of Applied Behavioral Science, 47*(3), 266–308.

Carey, M. P., & Forsyth, A. D. (2009). *Teaching Tip Sheet: Self-Efficacy.* American Psychological Association. https://www.apa.org/pi/aids/resources/education/self-efficacy

Carr, P. B., & Walton, G. M. (2014). Cues of working together fuel intrinsic motivation. *Journal of Experimental Social Psychology, 53,* 169–184.

Chang, E. (2001). *Optimism & Pessimism: Implications for Theory, Research, and Practice.* American Psychological Association.

Cooks-Campbell, A. (2022). *Toxic positivity at work: Examples and ways to manage it.* BetterUp. https://www.betterup.com/blog/toxic-positivity

Daimler, M. (2021). *Culture Starts & Ends With You: The Importance Of Defining Your Personal Culture.* Forbes. https://www.forbes.com/sites/melissadaimler/2021/02/04/culture-starts--ends-with-you-the-importance-of-defining-your-personal-culture/?sh=2a4118c16e33

Dalton-Smith, S. (2021). *The 7 types of rest that every person needs.* ideas.ted.com. https://ideas.ted.com/the-7-types-of-rest-that-every-person-needs/

Davis, T. (2023). *Self Development: The 9 Skills You Need to Improve Your Life*. Berkley Well-being Institute. https://www.berkeleywellbeing.com/self-development-the-9-skills-you-need-to-improve-your-life.html

DerSarkissian, C. (2024). *What to Know About Emotional Health*. WebMD. https://www.webmd.com/balance/what-to-know-about-emotional-health

Deutscher, A. (2023). *The Undeniable Link Between Well-Being And Productivity*. Forbes. https://www.forbes.com/sites/forbescoachescouncil/2023/08/22/the-undeniable-link-between-well-being-and-productivity/?sh=1ef08ee74280

DeWitt, P. M. (2022). *De-implementation: Creating the Space to Focus on What Works*. Corwin.

Duval, S., & Wicklund, R. A. (1972). *A Theory of Objective Self Awareness*. Academic Press.

Edmondson, A. (n.d.). *Psychological Safety*. https://amycedmondson.com/psychological-safety/

Erickson, E. P. G. (2023). *All About Optimism: Definition, Health Effects, and How to Boost Your Outlook*. Everyday Health. https://www.everydayhealth.com/emotional-health/optimism/guide/

Eurich, T. (2018). What Self-Awareness Really Is (and How to Cultivate It). *Harvard Business Review*. https://hbr.org/2018/01/what-self-awareness-really-is-and-how-to-cultivate-it

Feldman Barrett, L. (2018). The Science of Making Emotions. *Healthy Living Made Simple*. https://lisafeldmanbarrett.com/wp-content/uploads/sites/4/2020/11/ScienceOfMakingEmotions.pdf

Ferguson, K. (2023). *How to invest in your team early*. Substack. https://kirstinferguson.substack.com/p/how-to-invest-in-your-team-early

Finkelstein, D. (2023). *The Accountability Advantage: Play Your Best Game*.

Fisher, Cynthia. (2002). Real Time Affect at Work: A Neglected Phenomenon in Organisational Behaviour. *Australian Journal of Management, 2*.

Fleming, W. J. et al. (2024). Employee well-being outcomes from individual-level mental health interventions: Cross-sectional evidence from the United Kingdom. *Industrial Relations Journal*.

Gallup. (2024). *The Importance of Employee Recognition: Low Cost, High Impact*. https://www.gallup.com/workplace/236441/employee-recognition-low-cost-high-impact.aspx

Grant, A. (2017). *Originals: How Non-Conformists Move the World*. Penguin Books.

Gupta, S. (2023). *How to Improve Your Self-Worth and Why It's Important*. Verywellmind. https://www.verywellmind.com/what-is-self-worth-6543764

Hafner, M., van Stolk, C., Saunders, C., Krapels, J., & Baruch, B. (2015). *Health, wellbeing and productivity in the workplace: A Britain's Healthiest Company report*.

Iñiguez, L. (2023). *What is Team Culture and How to Build It*. Hirebook. https://www.hirebook.com/blog/what-is-team-culture-and-how-to-build-it

Kahn, W. A. (1990). Psychological conditions of personal engagement and disengagement at work. *Academy of Management Journal, 33*(4), 692–724.

Kanold, T. (2011). *The Five Disciplines of PLC Leaders*. Solution Tree.

Kelly, L. (2021). *7 Team Engagement Tips to Boost Teamwork and Performance.* peoplegoal. https://www.peoplegoal.com/blog/team-engagement

Learner Lab. (n.d.). *A Guide to Psychological Safety.* https://thelearnerlab.com/a-guide-to-psychological-safety/

Lencioni, P. (2002). *The Five Dysfunctions of a Team: A Leadership Fable.* Jossey-Bass.

Liu, S., Yu, B., Xu, C., Zhao, M. & Guo, J., (2022). Characteristics of Collective Resilience and Its Influencing Factors from the Perspective of Psychological Emotion: A Case Study of COVID-19 in China. *Int J Environ Res Public Health.* 19(22).

Lonczak, H. S. (2021). *Pessimism vs. Optimism: How Mindset Impacts Wellbeing.* PositivePsychology. https://positivepsychology.com/pessimism-vs-optimism

Maier, R. (2019). Self-Responsibility: Transformations. *American Behavioral Scientist,* 63(1), 27–42.

Miles, M. (2022.) *5 benefits of feedback – and why it matters.* BetterUp. https://www.betterup.com/blog/benefits-of-feedback

MiTraining. (n.d.). *What is the Difference Between Psychosocial and Psychological Safety?* https://mitraining.edu.au/blog/what-is-the-difference-between-psychosocial-and-psychological-safety

Mizell, H. (2010). *Why professional development matters.* Learning Forward. https://learningforward.org/wp-content/uploads/2017/08/professional-development-matters.pdf

Murthy, V. (2020). *Together: Why Social Connection Holds the Key to Better Health, Higher Performance, and Greater Happiness.* HarperCollins.

Neff, K. (2024). *What is self-compassion?* Self-Compassion. https://self-compassion.org/what-is-self-compassion

Nembhard, I. M., & Edmondson, A. C. (2006). Making it safe: The effects of leader inclusiveness and professional status on psychological safety and improvement efforts in health care teams. *Journal of Organizational Behavior,* 27(7), 941–966.

Parker, P. (2018). *The Art of Gathering: How We Meet and Why It Matters.* Penguin Books Limited.

Parker, P. (2022). *The New Rules of Gathering.* Priyaparker.com. https://www.priyaparker.com/the-new-rules-of-gathering

Perry, E. (2021). *The path to self-acceptance, paved through daily practice.* BetterUp. https://www.betterup.com/blog/self-acceptance

Psychology Today. (2023.) *Optimism.* https://www.psychologytoday.com/us/basics/optimism

Robbins, S. P., & Judge, T. A. (2012). *Organizational Behavior.* Pearson.

Roozeboom, M. B., & Schelvis, R. (2015). *Work engagement: drivers and effects.* European Agency for Safety and Health at Work.

Ryan, R. M., & Deci, E. L. (2001). On happiness and human potentials: A review of research on hedonic and eudaimonic well-being. *Annual Review of Psychology,* 52, 141–166.

Ryff, C. D., & Keyes, C. L. M. (1995). The structure of psychological well-being revisited. *Journal of Personality and Social Psychology,* 69(4), 719–727.

Safety Australia. (2023). *Understanding Psychological Safety and Psychosocial Risk*. https://safetyaustraliagroup.com.au/understanding-psychological-safety-and-psychosocial-risk/

Seligman, M. E. P. (2006). *Learned Optimism: How to Change Your Mind and Your Life*. Vintage Books.

Shahid, S., & Din, M. (2021). *Fostering Psychological Safety in Teachers: The Role of School Leadership, Team Effectiveness & Organizational Culture*. National University of Modern Languages, Pakistan.

Sikerbol, K. (2015). *Managing Emotional Reactions to Organizational Change*. Queens University. https://irc.queensu.ca/managing-emotional-reactions-to-organizational-change

Smith, T. et al. (2019). Teacher stress and its influence on student wellbeing: A longitudinal study. *Educational Psychology, 45*(2), 241–256.

State Government of Victoria. (n.d.). *Professional Practice: Effective Professional Learning*. https://www.education.vic.gov.au/Documents/school/teachers/teachingresources/practice/Professional_practice%20note_10_Effective_professional_learning.pdf

Stone, K. (2023). *Peer Feedback In Workplace*. Engagedly. https://engagedly.com/blog/the-importance-of-peer-feedback-at-workplace

Tobin, J. (2022). *7 Reasons To Build A Positive Workplace Culture*. Forbes. https://www.forbes.com/sites/forbesagencycouncil/2022/12/22/7-reasons-to-build-a-positive-workplace-culture/?sh=6a3c7b214c79

UNWC. (n.d.). *Self-worth*. https://uncw.edu/seahawk-life/health-wellness/counseling/self-help-resources/self-worth

Wilding, M. (2021). Re-Entry Stress Is Contagious. Here's How to Protect Yourself. *Harvard Business Review.* https://hbr.org/2021/10/re-entry-stress-is-contagious-heres-how-to-protect-yourself

World Health Organization. (2022). *Health and Well-being*. https://www.who.int/data/gho/data/major-themes/health-and-well-being

Wright, J. (2023). *Limiting beliefs: Are they paralysing your organisation?* Training Zone. https://www.trainingzone.co.uk/deliver/coaching/limiting-beliefs-are-they-paralysing-your-organisation

Acknowledgements

I never thought I would write one book, let alone two; having people who believe in you makes a significant difference. It's an odd thing putting my thoughts on paper in a space that for so long was overlooked. It's almost like opening up my diary, if that diary were work related.

I truly couldn't have done this again without a few key people who not only knew I could do it (sometimes more than I did), but also those who were incredibly patient with me, listened to me talk out my ideas asking many times 'Does this make sense?', and reading bits and pieces along the way.

This book really belongs to my publisher, Alicia, and editor, Brooke. Your unwavering commitment in allowing me to take my new learnings, ideas and experiences and turn them into a second book, and being patient while I spent 12 months crafting it, was incredibly supportive. I see both of you as my cheerleaders. While we don't connect often, when we do it's like you have been with me in person all the way.

Steven, the other half of me who by now is most likely ready to see this in print over multiple drafts and post-it notes spread out, once again, thank you. Not just for supporting but for sticking with your dreams so I can pursue mine.

To my siblings for being incredibly interested in the work I do and words I write. Support feels different when it is demonstrated in actions, such as reading a few chapters and giving feedback, asking meaningful questions and listening to my podcast so you can talk about my work with me. This doesn't go unnoticed. I love you all.

Fiona and Em, you both have been there. Despite being thousands of kilometres away, the space you each provide me to talk through ideas, share parts of me I am working through, and to be the sounding board with perspective I need, is so appreciated. I love you both.

My team. Corrina, without you, this wouldn't have happened. You have not only overhauled my business systems, allowed me to be more focused and productive, but also made space for this book in my calendar, making sure it was a priority. I owe a lot of this to you, you truly are amazing. And Amber, you have become an integral piece of my business. The tasks you have taken off me have given me space and capacity to get this book done. I appreciate the work you do.

Selena, you are one of a kind. Thank you for helping me unpack my ideas as I began this journey, and reminding me that even when I am filled with doubt, I know what I am doing. You truly are inspiring and I want to be just like you when I grow up.

To all of those who purchased my first book, thank you. Your support, encouragement and feedback fuelled me to write book two. I hope you like this one as much as you did the first.

Lastly, I'd like to thank myself. I know this seems odd and I don't think people usually do this in acknowledgements, but I think we should. Writing a book is hard work, and while the people above have supported, encouraged and championed me along the way, I have to do that for myself, too. Sometimes my inner critic was loud. To put my ideas, thoughts and beliefs into the chapters that make up this book, and not hold back, that's an accomplishment I need to acknowledge. I did that. So, Amy, thank you for not giving up, despite the self-doubt, you did it. Celebrate yourself.

About the Author

Amy Green is a leader and expert in improving staff wellbeing for schools, organisations and individuals. Amy is a published author, speaker, facilitator and coach who has a relatable approach to what can be a sensitive and personal topic. With a background in teaching, leadership and positive psychology, Amy brings a fresh take to this essential space.

Amy is dedicated to changing the way we view wellbeing in schools, empowering both schools and educators to move from reactive responses to embedded approaches. This means moving beyond morning teas and yoga classes to more strengthened, consistent strategies that focus on improving teacher wellbeing through building teacher capacity and enhancing school systems and processes. Amy's vision is to have schools across the globe making data-informed decisions that support teacher and staff wellbeing while building self and collective teacher efficacy.

Amy works with schools and educators in a variety of capacities, including school consultancy, professional development workshops and leadership, team and wellbeing mentoring.

www.ingramcontent.com/pod-product-compliance
Lightning Source LLC
Chambersburg PA
CBHW050357120526
44590CB00015B/1728